CONTENTS.

PAGE

CHAPTER I.
GENERAL RULES FOR MARKETING.

Meats—Poultry—Game—Fish—Vegetables—Fruit—Sweet Herbs **15**

CHAPTER II.
SOUP.

General Stock—Flavoring, thickening, and coloring Soups—Consommè—Vermicelli and Macaroni Soup—Rice and Tomato Soup—Scotch Broth without Meat—Scotch Broth with Meat—Spinach Soup—Sorrel Soup—Pea Soup—Lentil Soup **22**

CHAPTER III.
FISH.

Baked Blackfish—Broiled Shad with *Maître d'hotel* Butter—Fried Smelts—Fillet of Sole *au gratin*—Fish Chowder, St. James style—Club House Fish Cakes—Sardine Sandwiches—Warmed up Boiled Fish, with Dutch Sauce**31**

CHAPTER IV.
RELISHES.

Anchovies—Sardines—Pickled Herrings—Scalloped Oysters—Welsh Rarebit—Golden Buck—Mock Crab—English Bread and Butter—Epicurean Butter 37

CHAPTER V.
SIDE DISHES OR ENTRÉES.

Beef Steak, with Parisian Potatoes—Plain Rump Steak—Portuguese Beef—Bubble and Squeak—Stewed Kidneys—Haricot or Stew of Mutton—Epigramme of Lamb with Piquante Sauce—Spanish Sauce—Kromeskys with Spanish Sauce—Sheep's Tongues with Spinach—Broiled Sheep's Kidneys—Liver Rolls—Fried Brains with Tomato Sauce—Calf's Liver larded—Blanquette of Veal—Stuffed Breast of Veal—Pork Cutlets with Robert Sauce—Pork Chops with Curry—Broiled Pigs' Feet—English Pork Pie—Fried Chicken, Spanish Style—Chicken Fricassee—Grilled Fowl—Minced Chicken with Macaroni—Broiled Pigeons—Salmi of Duck—Civet of Hare—Jugged Hare—Stuffed Eggs—How to make Omelettes—Plain Omelette—Omelette with fine Herbs—Omelette with Ham—Omelette with Oysters—Omelette with Mushrooms—Spanish Omelette—Oriental Omelette—Omelette with Preserves—How to cook Macaroni—Macaroni with Béchamel Sauce—Macaroni

Milanaise Style—Macaroni with Tomato Sauce—Timbale of Macaroni, with Vanilla Cream Sauce **41**

CHAPTER VI.
LARGE ROASTS.

Roast Beef with Yorkshire Pudding—Roast Loin of Veal stuffed—Roast Lamb with Mint Sauce—Roast Pork with Apple Sauce—Roast Turkey with Cranberry Sauce—Roast Chicken with Duchesse Potatoes—Roast Duck with Watercresses—Roast Goose with Onion Sauce—Roast Wild Duck—Roast Partridge with Bread Sauce **68**

CHAPTER VII.
BOILED MEATS.

Leg of Mutton with Caper Sauce—Boiled Ham with Madeira Sauce—*À la mode* Beef—Boiled Fowl with Oyster Sauce **78**

CHAPTER VIII.
SALADS AND SALAD SAUCES.

Spring Salad—Watercress Salad—Mint Salad—Cauliflower Salad—Dandelion Salad—Asparagus Salad—Shad-roe Salad—Green Pea Salad—Orange Salad—Spinach Salad—Tomato Salad—Nasturtium Salad—Cream Dressing—English Salad Sauce—Remolade—Sweet Sauce—Piquante Salad Sauce

—Green Remolade—Oil Sauce—Ravigote Sauce—Egg Dressing—Anchovy Salad Sauce—Swiss Dressing—Spring Dressing—Mayonnaise—Hot Salad Sauce—Romaine Salad Dressing **83**

CHAPTER IX.
VEGETABLES.

Asparagus with Melted Butter—Green Peas—String Beans—Baked Beets—Brussels Sprouts—Stuffed Cabbage—Red Cabbage—Baked Cauliflower—Baked Turnips—Glazed Onions—Mushroom Pudding—Boiled Potatoes—Lyonnaise Potatoes—Stuffed Potatoes—Potato Snow—Bermuda Potatoes—Broiled Potatoes—Saratoga Potatoes—Broiled Tomatoes—Stuffed Tomatoes—Fried Beans—Ham and Beans—Kolcannon—Carrot Stew—Baked Mushrooms—Stuffed Lettuce—Stewed Parsnips **91**

CHAPTER X.
CHEAP DISHES WITHOUT MEAT.

Potato Soup—Crowdie—Peas-pudding—Red Herrings with Boiled Potatoes—Oatmeal Porridge—Cheese Pudding—Polenta—Fish Pudding—Lentils—Stewed Lentils—Fried Lentils—Norfolk Dumplings—Salt Cod with Parsnips—Pickled Mackerel—Potato Pudding **101**

CHAPTER XI.
CHEAP DISHES WITH MEAT.

Three Dishes from a Neck of Mutton—Barley Broth with Vegetables—Mutton Stew—Fried Pudding—Neck of Pork Stuffed—Pigs' Feet Fried—Pigs' Tongue and Brains—Roast Tripe—Ragout of Haslet—Cock-a-leeky—Italian Cheese—Gammon Dumpling—Toad-in-the-hole—Bacon Roly-Poly—Baked Ox-heart—Tripe and Onions—Peas and Bacon—Pot-au-Feu—Ragout of Mutton **107**

CHAPTER XII.
THE CHILDREN'S CHAPTER.

Oatmeal Porridge—A good Breakfast—Stewed Fruit—Ripe Currants—Blackberry Jam—Baked Fruit—Broiled Chops—Beefsteak—Broiled Chicken—Boiled Eggs—Baked Potatoes—Boiled Potatoes—Apple Cake—Fruit Farina—Plain Cookies—Plain Gingerbread—Strawberry Shortcake—Apple Custar **116**

CHAPTER XIII.
COOKERY FOR INVALIDS.

Gruels—Arrowroot Gruel—Arrowroot Jelly—Arrowroot Wine Jelly—Calf's-foot Jelly—Sago Gruel—Sago Milk—Tapioca Jelly—Rice Caudle—Refreshing Drinks—Filtered Water—

Jelly Water—Flaxseed Lemonade—Barley Water—Nourishing Drinks—Iceland Moss—Chocolate—Egg Broth—Egg Tea—Very Strong Beef Tea—Quick Beef Tea—Farina Gruel—Nutritious Foods—Bread Jelly—Crackers and Marmalade—Chicken Jelly—Chicken Broth—Beefsteak Juice—Salmon Steak—Broiled Oysters **125**

CHAPTER XIV.
BREAD.

Aerated Homemade Bread—Homebrewed Yeast—Homemade Bread—Milk Bread—Rice Bread—Potato Bread—Pulled Bread—Baking Powder—Loaf Bread—Breakfast Rolls—Tea Biscuit—Finger Biscuit—Cream Breakfast Rolls—Breakfast Twist—How to freshen stale Bread—Toast **134**

CHAPTER I.

MARKETING.

In order to market intelligently and economically, we must bear in mind the three great divisions of foods generally accepted in their consideration, and endeavor to adapt them to the requirements of our households; if we remember that carbonaceous, or heat-giving foods, such as the inner part of the cereals, fat meat, milk, honey, liver, grapes, peas, beans, potatoes, beets, carrots, and parsnips, are the best diet for hard steady workers, and for invalids suffering from wasting diseases; that nitrogenous, or flesh-forming foods, such as lean meat, unbolted flour, oatmeal, eggs, cheese, cabbage, cauliflower, onions, spinach, asparagus, and artichokes, are most suitable for those who work rapidly but with intervals of rest; and that brain-workers should subsist chiefly on light and digestible articles, such as fish, oysters, fruits, game, and vegetables containing mineral salts in excess; we can arrange the daily marketing so as to give a pleasant variety and at the same time satisfy all appetites.

Buy only small quantities of perishable things such as green vegetables, fruit, fish, eggs, cream, and fresh butter; buy dry groceries and preserved stores in quantities large enough to entitle you to wholesale prices; and pay cash in order to avail yourself of the lowest market price. Make your purchases as early in the day as possible in order to secure a choice of fresh articles; and trade with respectable dealers who give full weight and honest measure.

Meats.—While meats are in season all the year, they are better at stated times; for instance, pork is prime in late autumn and winter; veal should be avoided in summer for sanitary reasons; and even our staples, beef and mutton, vary in quality. The flesh of healthy animals is hard and fresh colored, the fat next the skin is firm and thick, and the suet or kidney-fat clear white and abundant; if this fat is soft, scant and stringy, the animal has been poorly fed or overworked. Beef should be of a bright red color, well marbled with yellowish fat, and surrounded with a thick outside layer of fat;

poor beef is dark red, and full of gristle, and the fat is scant and oily. Mutton is bright red, with plenty of hard white fat; poor mutton is dull red in color, with dark, muddy-looking fat. Veal and pork should be bright flesh color with abundance of hard, white, semi-transparent fat; when the fat is reddish and dark, the meat is of an inferior quality; veal and pork should be eaten very fresh. When meat of any kind comes into the house it should be hung up at once in some cool, dark place, and left until wanted.

Poultry.—Fresh poultry may be known by its full bright eyes, pliable feet, and soft moist skin; the best is plump, fat, and nearly white, and the grain of the flesh is fine. The feet and neck of a young fowl are large in proportion to its size, and the tip of the breast-bone is soft, and easily bent between the fingers; the body of a capon is large, fat, and round, the head comparatively small, and the comb pale and withered; a young cock, has short, loose, soft spurs, and a long, full, bright red comb; old fowls have long, thin necks and feet, and the flesh on the legs and back has a purplish shade; chickens, capons, and fowls, are always in season.

Turkeys when good are white and plump, have full breasts and smooth legs, generally black, with soft, loose spurs; hen turkeys are smaller, fatter, and plumper, but of inferior flavor; full grown turkeys are the best for boning and boiling, as they do not tear in dressing; old turkeys have long hairs, and the flesh is purplish where it shows under the skin on the legs and back. About March they deteriorate in quality. Turkey-poults are tender, but lack flavor.

Young ducks and geese are plump, with light, semi-transparent fat, soft breast-bone, tender flesh, leg joints which will break by the weight of the bird, fresh colored and brittle beaks, and windpipes that break when pressed between the thumb and fore-finger. They are best in fall and winter.

Young pigeons have light red flesh upon the breast, and full, fresh colored legs; when the legs are thin, and the breast is very dark, the birds are old. Squabs are tender and delicious.

The giblets of poultry consist of the head, neck, wings, feet, gizzard, heart, and liver; and make good soup, fricassees, pies, and various *entrées*, or side dishes.

Game.—Fine game birds are always heavy for their size; the flesh of the breast is firm and plump, the skin clear; and if a few feathers be plucked from the inside of the leg and around the vent, the flesh of freshly killed birds will be fat and fresh colored; if it is dark, and discolored, the game has been hung a long time. The wings of good ducks, geese, pheasants, and woodcock are tender to the touch; the tips of the long wing feathers of partridges are pointed in young birds, and round in old ones. Quail, snipe, and small birds should have full tender breasts.

Young rabbits and hares have short necks, thick knees, and forepaws which can be easily broken; old ones are very poor.

Buffalo meat is somewhat similar in appearance to beef, save that the flesh is darker, and the fat redder; it is tender and juicy when it has been kept long enough, say about two months in winter; the tongue, when cured, is excellent.

Venison should be tender, and very fat, or it will be dry and tasteless.

Bear meat, when fat and tender, is savory and nourishing.

Fish.—Sea fish, and those which live in both salt and fresh water, such as salmon, shad, and smelts, are the finest flavored; the muddy taste of some fresh water species can be overcome by soaking them in cold water and salt for two hours or more before cooking; all kinds are best just before spawning, the flesh becoming poor and watery after that period. Fresh fish have firm flesh, rigid fins, bright, clear eyes, and ruddy gills.

Oysters, clams, scallops, and mussels, should be eaten very fresh, as they soon lose their flavor after being removed from the shell.

Lobsters and crabs should be chosen by their brightness of color, lively movement, and great weight in proportion to their size.

Vegetables.—All juicy vegetables should be very fresh and crisp; and if a little wilted, can be restored by being sprinkled with water and laid in a cool, dark place; all roots and tubers should be pared and laid in cold water an hour or more before using. Green vegetables are best just before they flower; and roots and tubers are prime from their ripening until spring germination begins.

Fruit.—All fruit should be purchased ripe and sound; it is poor economy to buy imperfect or decayed kinds, as they are neither satisfactory nor healthy eating; while the mature, full-flavored sorts are invaluable as food.

Sweet Herbs.—Sweet and savory herbs are absolutely indispensable to good cooking; they give variety and savory flavors to any dish into which they enter, and are nearly all of some decided sanitary use; the different kinds called for in the various receipts further on in this work can be bought at almost any grocery store, or in the market; but we advise our readers to obtain seeds from some good florist and make little kitchen gardens of their own, even if the space planted be only a box of mould in the kitchen window. Sage, thyme, summer savory, sweet marjoram, tarragon, sweet basil, rosemary, mint, burnet, chervil, dill, and parsley, will grow abundantly with very little care; and when dried, and added judiciously to food, greatly improve its flavor. Parsley, tarragon and fennel, should be dried in May, June, and July, just before flowering; mint in June and July; thyme, marjoram, and savory in July and August; basil and sage in August and September; all herbs should be gathered in the sunshine, and dried by artificial heat; their flavor is best preserved by keeping them in air-tight tin cans.

Bay leaves can be procured at any drug store, or German grocery, at a very moderate expense; they have the flavor of laurel.

An excellent and convenient spice-salt can be made by drying, powdering, and mixing by repeated siftings the following ingredients: one quarter of an ounce each of powdered thyme, bay leaf, and pepper; one eighth of an ounce each of rosemary, marjoram, and cayenne pepper, or powdered capsicums; one half of an ounce each of powdered clove and nutmeg; to every four ounces of this powder add one ounce of salt, and keep the mixture in an air-tight vessel. One ounce of it added to three pounds of stuffing, or forcemeat of any kind, makes a delicious seasoning.

A bouquet of Sweet herbs.—The bouquet, or fagot, of sweet herbs, so often called for in foreign cooking, is made as follows: wash three or four sprigs of parsley, lay in their midst one sprig of thyme, and two bay leaves; fold the parsley over the thyme and bay leaves, tie it in a cork-shaped roll, about three inches long and one inch thick. The bouquet is used for seasoning soups, sauces, stews, and savory dishes in general, and is removed when the dish is served.

CHAPTER II.

SOUPS.

Soup is the most satisfactory and nourishing of all dishes when it is properly made. Its value depends upon what is put into it, but even in its most economical form it constitutes a hearty meal when eaten with bread and vegetables. It can be made from the merest scraps and trimmings of meat; from the heads, tails, and feet of animals; from the bones and skin of fish; and from cereals and vegetables alone. Pot liquor in which meat has been boiled should always be saved and used for soup the next day, when by the removal of all fat, by careful skimming, and the addition of a few vegetables or some dumplings, rice, or macaroni, it will make a palatable broth. Experiments made by French chemists prove that the delicacy and richness of soup may be increased by first soaking the meat in tepid water enough to cover it, and adding this to the second water in which the meat is put over the fire, just as it reaches the boiling point.

1. **General Stock.**—Part I.—Where there is a family of any size it is well to keep a clean pot or sauce-pan on the back of the stove to receive all the clean scraps of meat, bones, and remains of poultry and game, which are found in every kitchen; but vegetables should not be put into it, as they are apt to sour. The proper proportions for soup are one pound of meat and bone to one and a half quarts of cold water; the meat and bones to be well chopped and broken up, and put over the fire in cold water, being brought slowly to a boil, and carefully skimmed as often as any scum rises; and being maintained at a steady boiling point from two to six hours, as time permits; one hour before the stock is done, add to it one carrot and one turnip pared, one onion stuck with three cloves, and a bouquet of sweet herbs.

Part II.—When the soup is to be boiled six hours, two quarts of cold water must be allowed to every pound of meat; this will be reduced to one quart in boiling. Two gills of soup are usually allowed for each person at table when it is served as the first part of the dinner, and meats are to follow it. Care should be taken that the stock-pot boils slowly and constantly, from one side, as rapid and irregular boiling clouds and darkens the stock as much as imperfect skimming. Stock should never be allowed to cool in the stock-pot, but should be strained into an earthen jar, and left standing to cool uncovered, and all the fat removed, and saved to clarify for drippings; the stock is then ready to heat and use for soup, or gravy. When stock has been darkened and clouded by careless skimming and fast boiling, it can be clarified by adding to it one egg and the shell, mixed first with a gill of cold water, then with a gill of boiling soup, and stirring it briskly into the soup until it boils; then remove it to the back of the fire where it will not boil, and let it stand until the white and shell of the egg have collected the small particles clouding the soup; then strain it once or twice, until it looks clear.

2. **Flavoring, thickening, and coloring soups.**—The flavor of soup stock may be varied by using in it a little ham, anchovy, sausage, sugar, or a calf's foot. Herbs in the sprig, and whole spices should be used in seasoning, as they can easily be strained out. All delicate flavors, and wine, should be added to soup just before serving it, unless the contrary is expressly directed in the receipt, because boiling would almost entirely evaporate them: one gill of wine is usually allowed to every three pints of soup.

Soups which precede a full dinner should be less rich than those which form the bulk of the meal. Corn starch, arrow root, and potato flour are better than wheat flour for thickening soup. The meal of peas and beans can be held in suspension by mixing together dry a tablespoonful of butter and flour, and stirring it into the soup; a quarter of a pint of peas, beans, or lentils, is sufficient to make a quart of thick soup. Two ounces of macaroni, vermicelli, pearl barley, sago, tapioca, rice, or oatmeal, are usually allowed for each quart of stock.

If you wish to darken soup use a teaspoonful of caramel; but avoid burnt flour, carrot, and onion, as all these give a bad flavor. Caramel can be made from the following receipt; melt half a pound of loaf sugar in a thick copper vessel, stirring it frequently with a wooden spoon, and boiling it slowly until it assumes a rich brown color, but do not let it burn; when brown enough add one quart of cold water, stir well, and boil gently at the side of the fire for twenty minutes; then cool, strain, and bottle tight. In using the caramel add it just as you are about to serve the soup, or sauce colored with it.

3. **Clear Soup, or Consommé.** (*Two quarts for eight persons.*)—This is made by straining two quarts of stock, which has been cooled and freed from fat, through a piece of flannel or a napkin until it is bright and clear; if this does not entirely clear it, use an egg, as directed for clarifying soup; then season it to taste with salt, using at first a teaspoonful, and a very little fine white pepper, say a quarter of a saltspoonful; and color it to a bright straw color with caramel, of which a scant teaspoonful will be about the proper quantity. *Consommé* is sent to the table clear, but sometimes a deep dish containing poached eggs, one for each person, with enough *consommé* to cover them, accompanies it.

4. **Poached Eggs for Consommé.**—Break the eggs, which should be very fresh, into a deep sauce-pan half full of boiling water, seasoned with a teaspoonful of salt, and half a gill of vinegar; cover the sauce-pan, and set it on the back part of the fire until the whites of the eggs are firm; then lift them separately on a skimmer, carefully trim off the rough edges, making each egg a regular oval shape, and slip them off the skimmer into a bowl of hot, but not boiling water, where they must stand for ten minutes before serving.

5. **Vermicelli and Macaroni Soup.**—These soups are both made as for *consommé*; and to every quart of stock is added two ounces of one of these pastes blanched as follows. Put the paste into plenty of boiling water, with one tablespoonful of salt to each quart of water, and boil until tender enough to pierce with the finger nail; then drain it, and put it in cold water until required for use, when it should be placed in the two quarts of hot soup long enough to heat thoroughly before serving.

6. **Rice and Tomato Soup.**—Strain, and pass through a sieve with a wooden spoon, one pint of tomatoes, either fresh or canned, stir them into two quarts of good, clear stock, free from fat; season it with a teaspoonful of salt, and quarter of a saltspoonful of pepper; taste, and if the seasoning seems deficient add a little more, but do not put in too much for general liking, for more can easily be added, but none can be taken out. Add four

ounces of rice, well washed in plenty of cold water, and boil the soup slowly for three quarters of an hour before serving.

7. **Scotch Broth without Meat.**—Steep four ounces of pearl barley over night in cold water, and wash it well in fresh water; cut in dice half an inch square, six ounces of yellow turnip, six ounces of carrot, four ounces of onion, two ounces of celery, (or use in its place quarter of a saltspoonful of celery seed;) put all these into two and a half quarts of boiling water, season with a teaspoonful of salt, quarter of a saltspoonful of pepper, and as much cayenne as you can take up on the point of a very small pen-knife blade; boil slowly for two hours; then stir in quarter of a pound of oatmeal, mixed to a smooth batter with cold water, see if seasoning be correct, add two or three grates of nutmeg, and boil half an hour. Meantime, cut two slices of bread in half inch dice, fry light brown in hot fat, and lay the bits in the soup tureen; when the soup is ready pour it over them, and serve. This soup is very rich and nutritious, and should be served with light dinners.

8. **Scotch Broth with Meat.**—Put four ounces of barley to soak in warm water. From two pounds of the shoulder of mutton, cut the lean meat in dice half an inch square; cut up the rest in small pieces and make a stock as directed in receipt *No. 1., Part I.*, using two and a half quarts of water, and boiling and skimming for two hours; at the end of an hour and a half put the dice of meat into a sauce-pan with two ounces of butter, and fry them brown; stir in one ounce of flour; cut in dice six ounces each of yellow turnip and carrot, chop four ounces of onion, and put these with the meat; add the barley, and the stock strained, season with a teaspoonful of salt, and quarter of a saltspoonful of pepper, and simmer one hour. Then serve with a tablespoonful of chopped parsley sprinkled in the soup.

9. **Spinach Soup.**—Blanch two quarts of spinach, by putting it into a large pot full of boiling water, with two tablespoonfuls of salt, cover until it boils up once; then remove the cover, and with a wooden spoon press the spinach under water as fast as it rises to the surface; boil it steadily until it is tender enough to pierce easily with the finger nail; then drain it; run plenty of cold water from the faucet over it, while it is still in the colander; drain it again, chop it fine, and pass it through a kitchen sieve with the aid of a wooden spoon; boil two quarts of milk, add the spinach to it, thicken it by stirring in one tablespoonful of corn starch dissolved in cold milk; season it with one

teaspoonful of salt, quarter of a saltspoonful of white pepper, and the same of nutmeg; and serve it as soon as it boils up.

10. **Sorrel Soup.**—Put one pint of sorrel into a sauce-pan with a dessertspoonful of salt, and one gill of cold water; cover it, and cook until it is tender enough to pierce with the finger nail, then drain, wash it well with cold water, chop it and pass it through the kitchen sieve with a wooden spoon; meantime brown half an ounce of chopped onion in a sauce-pan with one ounce of butter; add one ounce of flour, and stir till brown; then add two quarts of hot water, or hot water and stock, and the sorrel, and season with one teaspoonful of salt, quarter of a saltspoonful of pepper, and the same of nutmeg; mix the yolks of two eggs with two tablespoonfuls of cold water, add to them half a pint of boiling soup, and gradually stir the mixture into the soup, boiling it a minute after it is thoroughly blended; meantime cut two slices of bread into half inch dice, fry them brown in smoking hot fat, drain them free from grease on a napkin, put them into a soup tureen, pour the soup on them, and serve at once.

11. **Pea Soup.**—Use half a pint of dried peas for thick soup, or one pint for a *purée*, to two quarts of stock or cold water. Bring slowly to a boil; add a bone or bit of ham, one turnip and one carrot peeled, one onion stuck with three cloves, and simmer three hours stirring occasionally to prevent burning; then pass the soup through a sieve with the aid of a potato masher; and if it shows any sign of settling stir into it one tablespoonful each of butter and flour mixed together dry; this will hold the meal in solution; meantime fry some dice of stale bread, about two slices, cut half an inch square, in hot fat, drain them on a napkin, and put them in the bottom of the soup tureen in which the pea soup is served.

12. **Lentil Soup.**—The seed of the lentil tare commonly cultivated in France and Germany as an article of food, ranks nearly as high as meat, as a valuable food, being capable of sustaining life and vigor for a long time; this vegetable is gradually becoming known in this country, from the use of it by our French and German citizens; and from its nutritive value it deserves to rank as high as our favorite New England beans. For two quarts of lentil soup half a pint of yellow lentils should be well washed, and put to boil in three pints of cold water, with a small carrot, an onion, two sprigs of parsley, and two bay leaves, and boiled gently until the lentils are soft

enough to break easily between the fingers; every half hour one gill of cold water should be added, and the lentils again raised to the boiling point, until they are done; they should then be drained in a colander, and passed through a sieve with a wooden spoon, using enough of the liquor to make them pass easy, and mixed with the rest of the soup; it is then ready to simmer for half an hour, and serve hot; with dice of fried bread half an inch square, like those used for pea soup. These dice of fried bread are called *Condé* crusts.

CHAPTER III.

FISH.

When fish is rather deficient in flavor, a little vinegar rubbed over the skin; and a few sweet herbs boiled with it will greatly improve it. For boiling, large fish should be placed on the fire in cold water, and small ones in hot water; both are done when the fins pull out easily. Fish soup is the most economical of all fish dishes; baked fish the second best; broiled fish retains nearly all its nourishment; and boiled fish is the poorest of all. The following technical terms are used to denote different methods of cooking fish: to dress fish *à la Hollandaise* is to boil it in sea water; *à l'eau de sel*, in salt and water; *au court bouillon*, with cold water, white wine or vinegar, sweet herbs, soup vegetables, lemon, and whole spices; *à la bonne eau*, with sweet herbs and cold water; *au bleu*, in equal quantities of red wine and cold water, highly flavored with spices and aromatic herbs.

13. **Boiled Cod with Oyster Sauce.**—Lay two pounds of cod in enough cold water to cover it, with a tablespoonful of salt, for an hour or more before cooking; then put it to boil in three quarts of cold water, with two tablespoonfuls of salt; as soon as the fish is done, set the kettle containing it off the fire, and let the fish stand in it until you are ready to use it; meantime put a pint of oysters on the fire to boil in their own liquor; as soon as they boil drain them, and put the liquor again on the fire to boil; mix together in a sauce-pan over the fire one ounce of butter and one ounce of flour, as soon as it bubbles, gradually pour in the boiling oyster liquor, and stir with an egg whip until the sauce is quite smooth; season with half a teaspoonful of salt, an eighth of a saltspoonful of pepper, and the same of nutmeg; and add the oysters. Take up the fish, serve it on a napkin, and send it to the table with a bowl containing the oyster sauce.

14. **Baked Blackfish.**—Have a fish weighing from two to two and a half pounds cleaned by the fishmonger; rub it well with a handful of salt, to remove the slime peculiar to this fish, wash it well, and wipe it with a clean, dry cloth; stuff it with the following forcemeat. Put four ounces of stale

bread to soak in sufficient luke-warm water to cover it; meantime fry one ounce of chopped onion in one ounce of butter until it is light brown; then wring the bread dry in a clean towel, put it into the onion with two tablespoonfuls of chopped parsley, one ounce of salt pork chopped fine, one teaspoonful of chopped capers or pickles, one teaspoonful of salt, quarter of a saltspoonful of white pepper, and one gill of broth or hot water; stir until it is scalding hot, when it will cleave from the bottom and sides of the saucepan; then stuff the fish with it, and lay it in a dripping pan on one ounce of carrot and one ounce of onion sliced, one bay leaf and two sprigs of parsley; cover the fish with slices of salt pork, season it with a saltspoonful of salt, and one fourth that quantity of pepper, and bake it in a moderate oven for half an hour, basting it occasionally with a little butter, or stock. When it is done, put it on a dish to keep hot while you prepare a sauce by straining the drippings in the pan, and adding to them one tablespoonful each of walnut catsup, Worcestershire sauce, chopped capers, and chopped parsley. Pour a little of this sauce in the bottom of the dish under the fish, and serve the rest with it in a bowl.

15. **Broiled Shad with Maître d'hotel butter.**—Choose a medium sized shad, weighing about three pounds, have it cleaned and split down the back; turn it occasionally for an hour or more, in a marinade made of one tablespoonful of salad oil, or melted butter, one of vinegar, a saltspoonful of salt, and quarter of a saltspoonful of pepper; lay it on a gridiron, rubbed with a little butter to prevent sticking, broil it slowly, doing the inside first, and, after laying it on a hot dish, spread over it some *maître d'hotel* butter.

16. **Maître d'hotel Butter.**—Mix together cold, one ounce of butter, a tablespoonful of chopped parsley, a teaspoonful of lemon juice, and quarter of a saltspoonful of pepper; and spread it over the broiled shad. This butter is excellent for any kind of broiled fish, or for steaks.

17. **Fried Smelts, French Style.**—Carefully wipe two pounds of cleaned smelts with a dry cloth; dip them in milk, then roll them in finely powdered cracker crumbs, next in an egg beaten with a saltspoonful of salt, and quarter of a saltspoonful of pepper, and then again in cracker crumbs; fry them in enough smoking hot fat to cover them, until they are golden brown; take them from the fat with a skimmer, lay them on a napkin, or a piece of

paper to absorb all fat; and serve them laid in rows with a few quarters of lemon on the side of the dish.

18. **Fillet of Sole au gratin.**—Choose two flounders weighing about three pounds. Lay them on the table with the dark side uppermost; with a sharp, thin-bladed knife cut down to the back bone, following the dark line in the middle of the fish; then turn the edge of the knife outward, and cut towards the fins, keeping the blade flat against the bone, and removing one quarter of the flesh of the fish in a single piece; proceed in the same way until you have eight fillets; carefully cut the skin from them; season them with salt and pepper, lay them on a buttered dish suitable to send to table, sprinkle them thickly with sifted cracker crumbs, and a little grated Parmesan, or any rich, dry cheese; put a few bits of butter over them, using not more than an ounce in all, and brown them in a quick oven. Serve them as soon as they are nicely browned. This is a very savory and delicate dish, requiring some practice to do nicely, but comparatively inexpensive, and well worth all trouble taken in making it.

19. **St. James Fish Chowder.**—Put half a pound of sliced salt pork in the bottom of a deep sauce-pan and fry it brown; take it out, and put in layers of potatoes, onions and fish sliced, seasoning each layer plentifully with salt and pepper; using about three pounds of fish, and a quart each of potatoes and onions; cover with cold water, bring gradually to a boil, and cook slowly for thirty minutes; then add two pounds of sea-biscuits soaked for five minutes in warm water, and boil five minutes longer and serve. This receipt calls for the addition of half a pint of port wine, and a bottle of champagne to be added to the chowder just before serving; but it is quite good enough without, and far less expensive.

20. **Club House Fish Cakes.**—Wash and boil one quart of potatoes, putting them on the fire in cold water enough to cover them, and a tablespoonful of salt. Put one and a half pounds of salt codfish on the fire in plenty of cold water, and bring it slowly to a boil; as soon as it boils throw off that water, and put it again on the fire in fresh cold water; if the fish is very salt change the water a third time. Free the fish from skin and bone; peel the potatoes, mash them through a colander with a potato masher, season them with quarter of a saltspoonful of pepper and an ounce of butter; add the yolks of two eggs, and the fish; mix well, and make into cakes, using a little flour to

prevent sticking to the hands. Fry them golden brown in enough smoking hot fat to nearly cover them; observe that in frying any article of food it will not soak fat if the latter be hot enough to carbonize the outside at once, and smoking hot fat will do that.

21. **Sardine Sandwiches.**—Butter sixteen thin slices of bread on both sides, put between each two a very thin layer of sardines, sprinkled with a little lemon juice, and brown them in a quick oven.

22. **Warmed up boiled fish, with Dutch Sauce.**—Put the cold fish on the fire in plenty of cold water and salt, and let it come slowly to a boil; meantime make a sauce for it as follows.

23. **Dutch Sauce.**—Put one ounce of butter, and one ounce of flour in a sauce-pan over the fire, and stir constantly until it bubbles; then add gradually one gill of boiling water, remove the sauce from the fire, stir in the yolks of three eggs, one at a time, add one saltspoonful of dry mustard; add one tablespoonful of vinegar and three of oil, gradually, drop by drop, stirring constantly till smooth. When the fish is warmed take it up carefully without breaking and serve with the Dutch sauce in a boat.

CHAPTER IV.

RELISHES.

The dishes known as relishes are usually eaten at dinner just after the soup or fish; they are in reality the restorers of appetite; they are usually cold, and are sent to the table on small oval dishes, or ornamental boats.

24. **Anchovies.** (*One for each person.*)—The best anchovies are small and plump, with white scales, and dark red pickle; they are prepared for the table by soaking two hours in cold water, taking out the back-bone, removing the scales and some of the small bones, and serving them with oil or vinegar in a suitable dish, or pickle shell.

25. **Sardines.** (*One for each person.*)—Sardines are served by wiping them, and serving them on a small dish with quarters of lemons beside them.

26. **Pickled Herrings.** (*One for each person.*)—These are served in a boat with a few capers, and a little chopped parsley sprinkled over them.

27. **Scalloped Oysters.** (*One shell for each person.*)—Blanch one quart of oysters by bringing just to a boil in their own liquor, then strain them, saving the liquor, and keeping it hot; wash them in cold water and drain them; mix one ounce of butter and one ounce of flour together in a sauce-pan over the fire; as soon as it is smooth gradually stir in one pint of the oyster liquor, which must be boiling; season the sauce with half a teaspoonful of salt, and quarter of a saltspoonful each of white pepper and nutmeg; put the oysters into it to heat, while you thoroughly wash eight or ten deep oystershells with a brush; fill them with the oysters, dust them thickly with bread crumbs; put a small bit of butter on each one, and brown them in a quick oven; they should be sent to the table laid on a napkin neatly folded on a platter.

28. **Welsh Rarebit.**—Grate one pound of rich cheese, mix it over the fire with one gill of ale, working it smooth with a spoon; season it with a saltspoonful of dry mustard; meantime make two large slices of toast, lay

them on a hot dish, and as soon as the cheese is thoroughly melted, pour it over the toast and send it to the table at once.

29. **Golden Buck.**—Prepare the cheese and toast as in receipt No. 28; cut the toast in eight pieces; while the cheese is melting poach eight eggs, by dropping them gently into plenty of boiling water containing a teaspoonful of salt, and half a gill of vinegar; as soon as the whites are firm, take them carefully out on a skimmer, trim off the edges, and slip them again into warm water, while you divide the cheese on the pieces of toast; then lay an egg on each piece, and serve at once. The success of the dish depends upon having the eggs, cheese, and toast ready at the same moment, putting them together very quickly, and serving them before they cool.

30. **Mock Crab.**—Break up half a pound of soft, rich cheese with a fork, mix with it a teaspoonful of dry mustard, a saltspoonful of salt, half a saltspoonful of pepper, and a dessertspoonful of vinegar; serve it cold, with a plate of thin bread and butter, or crisp crackers.

31. **English bread and butter.**—Cut an even slice off a large loaf of fresh homemade bread; butter the cut end of the loaf thinly, then hold it against the side with the left hand and arm, and with a sharp, thin knife, cut an even slice not more than an eighth of an inch thick; a little practice, and a steady grasp of bread and knife, will enable any one to produce regular whole slices; fold each one double, with the butter inside; and cut as many as you require; serve them on a clean napkin, and send them to the table with any other of the above relishes.

32. **Cheese Straws.**—Sift six ounces of flour on the pastry board, make a hole or well in the centre; into this well put two tablespoonfuls of cream, three ounces of grated Parmesan, or any rich dry cheese, four ounces of butter, half a teaspoonful of salt, quarter of a teaspoonful of white pepper, and the same quantity of grated nutmeg, together with as much cayenne as you can take up on the point of a very small pen-knife blade; mix all these ingredients with the tips of the fingers, to a firm paste, knead it well, roll it out an eighth of an inch thick; and with a sharp knife, or pastry jagger, cut it in straws about eight inches long, and quarter of an inch wide; lay the strips carefully on a buttered tin, and bake them light straw color in a moderate oven. These cheese straws make a delicious accompaniment to salad.

33. **Epicurean Butter.**—Bone and skin four anchovies or sardines, and chop them fine; chop a tablespoonful of chives, and the same quantity of tarragon leaves, four small green pickles, the yolks of two hard boiled eggs; mix with these ingredients, a level teaspoonful of French mustard, a saltspoonful of salt, and two ounces of sweet butter; pass them all through a fine sieve with the aid of a wooden spoon; put it on the ice to cool, and then mould it in balls the size of a walnut, by rolling small lumps between two little wooden paddles; serve it with crackers and cheese.

These receipts are given because many persons call for them; the author begs leave to accompany them with the assurance that a prolonged diet of any of them will produce a well grounded dyspepsia in a very moderate length of time.

CHAPTER V.

SIDE DISHES, OR ENTRÉES.

The multitude of dishes known as *entrées*, represent to a great extent the economical use of food for which the French are so celebrated; they are based upon the principles of suitable combination. Usage has classed certain sorts of food together as fit adjuncts; for instance, *bon vivants* instruct us that white sauces and light wines are the best accompaniments for fish, poultry, and the white meats; and that brown sauces, and rich, heavy wines, naturally follow with the dark meats and game. These general principles readily apply to the preparation of the numberless made dishes which are the glory of European cookery, and which transform the remains of an ordinary meat breakfast into a delicious luncheon, or an inviting side-dish for dinner. The fact that the secret of all good cookery is economy, must be our apology for treating this division of our subject at some length; and we beg our readers to test our receipts before accusing us of attempting to introduce obnoxious and difficult culinary methods into American kitchens.

34. **How Meat should be Broiled.**—In broiling all meats, you must remember that the surface should not be cut or broken any more than is absolutely necessary; that the meat should be exposed to a clear, quick fire, close enough to sear the surface without burning, in order to confine all its juices; if it is approached slowly to a poor fire, or seasoned before it is cooked, it will be comparatively dry and tasteless, as both of these processes are useful only to extract and waste those precious juices which contain nearly all the nourishing properties of the meat.

35. **Parisian Potatoes.**—Pare and cut one quart of raw potatoes in balls the size of a walnut, reserving the trimmings to use for mashed potatoes; put the balls over the fire in plenty of cold water and salt, and boil them until just tender enough to pierce easily with a fork; which will be in about fifteen minutes; drain them, lay them on a towel a moment to dry them, and then brown them in enough smoking hot lard to immerse them entirely;

when they are brown take them up in a colander, and sprinkle them with a saltspoonful of salt, and a teaspoonful of chopped parsley.

36. **To broil a Beefsteak.**—Rub the bars of the gridiron smooth, and then grease them slightly; lay on a sirloin steak weighing about three pounds; put the gridiron over a hot fire; if the fire is not clear throw a handful of salt into it to clear it; broil the steak, turning it frequently so that it cannot burn, until it is done to the required degree; do not cut into it to ascertain this, but test it by pressing the tips of the fingers upon it; if it spring up again after the pressure is removed it is done rare; if it remains heavy and solid it is well done; while it is broiling prepare a *maître d'hotel* butter according to receipt No. 16; spread it over the steak after you have laid it on a hot dish, and arrange the *Parisian potatoes* at the sides of the dish; send it to the table at once. After the proper cooking of a steak comes the immediate eating thereof, if it is to be found perfect.

37. **Plain Rump Steak.**—Broil three pounds of tender rump steak according to directions in receipt No. 36, put it on a hot dish, season it with a level teaspoonful of salt, and quarter of a saltspoonful of pepper, spread over it one ounce of butter, and lay two tablespoonfuls of grated horseradish on the side of the platter, and serve it hot, without delay.

38. **Portuguese Beef.**—Cut in thin shavings two pounds of cold beef, and put it into a sauce-pan with half a pint of any brown gravy, and heat it gradually; in another pan put one small onion chopped fine, the rind of one orange chopped, the juice, quarter of a saltspoonful of grated nutmeg, as much cayenne as can be taken up on the point of a very small pen-knife blade, and one gill of port wine; boil these ingredients rapidly until the liquid is reduced one half, and then mix them with the beef; fry in hot fat some slices of bread, cut in the shape of hearts, about two inches long and one inch wide, pile the beef in a mound on a hot dish, lay the *croutons* of fried bread around it, and serve it hot.

39. **Bubble and Squeak.**—Cut about two pounds of cold meat in neat slices, put them into a pan with an ounce of butter, and brown them; at the same time chop one head of tender cabbage, without the stalks, put it into a sauce-pan with two ounces of butter, a saltspoonful of salt, and quarter of a saltspoonful of pepper, and stir it occasionally over the fire until it is quite

tender; when both are done, lay the slices of beef in the centre of a hot dish, and arrange the cabbage around it; serve it hot.

40. **Stewed Kidneys.**—Cut one large beef kidney in thin slices about an inch long; fry two ounces of onion in one ounce of butter, until pale yellow; add the kidney, fry or rather *sauter* it, for about five minutes, shaking the pan frequently to prevent burning; then stir in one ounce and a half of flour, season with one saltspoonful of salt, a quarter of a saltspoonful of pepper, and the same of powdered sweet herbs made as directed on page 20, and one gill of boiling water; cook ten minutes longer; meantime make eight heart-shaped *croutons* of bread, as directed in receipt No. 38; add one gill of Madeira wine to the kidneys, pour them on a hot dish, sprinkle them with a teaspoonful of chopped parsley, arrange the *croutons* around the border of the dish, and serve hot at once. The success of this dish depends on serving it while the kidneys are tender; too much cooking hardens them; and they must not be allowed to stand after they are done, or they deteriorate.

41. **Haricot or Stew of Mutton.**—Trim a neck of mutton, weighing about two pounds, of all superfluous fat, cut it into cutlets, put them in a deep sauce-pan with one ounce of butter, and fry them brown; pour off all fat, add two ounces of flour, stir till brown, moisten with one quart and a half of stock, or water, and stir occasionally until the haricot boils; meantime cut one quart of carrots and turnips, half and half, in small balls, and add them, with one dozen button onions, a bouquet of sweet herbs, half a saltspoonful of pepper, and a teaspoonful of salt; simmer for one hour; take up the cutlets with a fork, skim out the vegetables, and remove the bouquet; lay the cutlets in a wreath on a hot dish, place the vegetables in the centre, and strain the gravy over all. Green peas, new turnips, or new potatoes, may replace the first named vegetables. The dish should always be sent to the table hot.

42. **Epigramme of Lamb, with Piquante Sauce.**—Boil a breast of young mutton, weighing from two to three pounds until tender, either in the stock-pot, or in hot water seasoned with salt, two cloves stuck in a small onion, and a bouquet of sweet herbs made as directed in the first chapter; when it is tender enough to permit the bones to be drawn out easily, take it up, lay it on a pan, put another, containing weights, on it, and press it until it is cold; then cut it in eight triangular pieces, about the size of a small cutlet; season them with salt and pepper; roll them first in sifted cracker dust, then in an

egg beaten with a tablespoonful of cold water, and again in cracker dust; fry them light brown in enough smoking hot fat to cover them.

43. **Piquante Sauce.**—While the lamb is frying, chop one tablespoonful of capers, two of shallot, or small, finely flavored onion, and the same quantity of green gherkins; place them over the fire in a sauce-pan with one gill of vinegar, two bay leaves, quarter of a saltspoonful of pepper, and the same of powdered thyme, and boil quickly until the vinegar is reduced to one third of its original quantity; then add half a pint of rich brown gravy of any kind, or of Spanish sauce, which may always be kept on hand; boil the sauce gently for five minutes, take out the bay leaves, and pour a little of the sauce on the bottom of a hot platter; when the pieces of breast are brown, take them up with a skimmer, and lay them on soft paper, or on a clean napkin for a moment, to free them from grease, and arrange them in a wreath on the platter containing the sauce; serve them at once, with the rest of the sauce in a gravy boat.

44. **Spanish Sauce.**—Fry one ounce of ham or bacon, cut in half-inch dice, with one ounce of fat; add to it, as soon as brown, two ounces of carrot sliced, two ounces of onion sliced; stir in two ounces of dry flour, and brown well; then add one quart of stock; or if none is on hand, one quart of water, and half a pound of lean meat chopped fine; season with a teaspoonful of salt, quarter of a saltspoonful of pepper, and a bouquet of sweet herbs, made as directed in the first chapter; simmer gently for an hour, skimming as often as any scum rises; then strain the sauce, add one gill of wine to it, and use it to dress any dark meat, game, or baked fish. This sauce will keep a week or longer, in a cool place.

45. **Kromeskys, with Spanish Sauce.**—Cut one pound of cold roast lamb, or mutton, in half inch dice; chop one ounce of onion, and fry it pale yellow in one ounce of butter; add one ounce of flour, and stir until smooth; add half a pint of Spanish sauce, or water, if no sauce is at hand, two tablespoonfuls of chopped parsley, one level teaspoonful of salt, one level saltspoonful of white pepper, half a saltspoonful of powdered herbs, as much cayenne as can be taken up on the point of a very small pen-knife blade, and the chopped meat; two ounces of mushrooms, slightly warmed with quarter of an ounce of butter, and a teaspoonful of lemon juice, improve the flavor of the *kromeskys* exceedingly; stir until scalding hot, add

the yolk of one raw egg, cook for two minutes, stirring frequently; and turn out to cool on a flat dish, slightly oiled, or buttered, to prevent sticking, spreading the minced meat about an inch thick; set away to cool while the batter is being made.

46. **Plain Frying Batter.**—Mix quarter of a pound of flour with the yolks of two raw eggs, a level saltspoonful of salt, half a saltspoonful of pepper, quarter of a saltspoonful of grated nutmeg, one tablespoonful of salad oil, (which is used to make the batter crisp,) and one cup of water, more or less, as the flour will take it up; the batter should be stiff enough to hold the drops from the spoon in shape when they are let fall upon it; now beat the whites of the two eggs to a stiff froth, beginning slowly, and increasing the speed until you are beating as fast as you can; the froth will surely come; then stir it lightly into the batter; heat the dish containing the meat a moment, to loosen it, and turn it out on the table, just dusted with powdered crackers; cut it in strips an inch wide and two inches long, roll them lightly under the palm of the hand, in the shape of corks, dip them in the batter, and fry them golden brown in smoking hot fat. Serve them on a neatly folded napkin. They make a delicious dish, really worth all the care taken in preparing them.

47. **Sheep's Tongues with Spinach.**—Boil eight sheep's tongues in the stock pot, or in hot water with a bouquet of sweet herbs, and a gill of vinegar, for about an hour, or until they are quite tender; then remove them from the stock, lay them on their sides on a flat dish, place over them another dish with weights on it, and allow them to cool: trim them neatly, put them into a sauce-pan with enough Spanish sauce, or brown gravy to cover them, and heat them gradually.

48. **To boil Spinach.**—Wash and trim one quart of green spinach, put it into a sauce-pan holding at least three quarts of boiling water, and three tablespoonfuls of salt, and boil it rapidly, with the cover off, until it is tender enough to pierce easily with the finger nail, which will be in from three to seven minutes, according to the age of the spinach; then drain it in a colander, wash it in cold water, thoroughly drain it again, and chop it very fine, or pass it through a sieve with a wooden spoon; put it into a sauce-pan with enough Spanish sauce or brown gravy to moisten it, season it with a saltspoonful of salt, and half that quantity of white pepper, and heat it until

it steams; arrange the tongues in a wreath on a hot platter, put the spinach in the centre, and pour the gravy in which the tongues were heated, over them. Serve hot at once.

49. **Broiled Sheep's Kidneys.**—Split eight kidneys lengthwise, skin them, lay them for half an hour in a dish containing a tablespoonful of salad oil, the same of some spiced vinegar, or table sauce, and a saltspoonful of salt and pepper mixed equally; turn them frequently; then roll them in cracker dust, lay them on a greased gridiron, and broil them, the inside first; when done brown, place them on a hot dish, with a small piece of *maître d'hotel* butter in each, made according to receipt No. 16, and send them hot to the table.

50. **Liver Rolls.**—Cut two sheep's livers in slices half an inch thick; season them with salt and pepper; spread over each a layer of sausage meat as thick as the liver, season that, roll each slice up, and tie it in place with a string; on the bottom of a baking pan put one ounce of carrot, and one ounce of onion sliced, two bay leaves, one sprig of thyme, three of parsley, and an ounce of salt pork sliced; lay the liver on these, put over each roll a tablespoonful of brown gravy, or Spanish sauce, and bake them in a moderate oven about forty minutes, or until they are thoroughly cooked; lay them on a hot platter, add a gill of stock or water to the pan they were baked in, stir the vegetables about in it, and strain it over the liver. Serve at once.

51. **Fried Brains with Tomato Sauce.**—Lay four pieces of calf's brains in cold water and salt for one hour, to draw out the blood; meantime begin a tomato sauce as directed below; carefully remove the outer skin without breaking the brains; put them over the fire in enough cold water to cover them, with half a gill of vinegar, two bay leaves, a sprig of parsley, and an onion stuck with three cloves; bring them to a boil, and simmer slowly for ten minutes; take them up carefully, and lay them in cold water and salt to cool. When cool, cut each one in two pieces, roll them first in cracker dust, then in one raw egg beaten with a tablespoonful of cold water, then again in cracker dust, and fry them in plenty of smoking hot fat; as soon as they are golden brown take them up on a skimmer, and lay them on a soft paper or napkin to absorb all fat, and then arrange on a platter containing half a pint of tomato sauce.

52. **Tomato Sauce.**—Put into a thick sauce-pan half a can, or one pint of tomatoes, one ounce of carrot, and the same quantity of onion sliced, one ounce of salt pork cut in small bits, a bouquet of sweet herbs, made as directed in Chapter first, four cloves, one clove of garlic, if it is liked, one teaspoonful of salt, quarter of a saltspoonful of pepper, and a gill of stock, gravy, or water; simmer slowly one hour, and pass through a sieve with a wooden spoon. This is an excellent sauce for any breaded side dish.

53. **Calf's Liver larded.**—The operation of larding is done by passing strips of larding pork, which is firm, white, fat pork, cut two inches long, and quarter of an inch square, in rows along the surface of a liver, placing the strips of pork in the split end of a larding needle, and with it taking a stitch about a quarter of an inch deep and one inch long in the surface of the liver, and leaving the ends of the pork projecting equally; the rows must be inserted regularly, the ends of the second coming between the ends of the first, and so on, until the surface is covered; the liver is then laid in a dripping pan on one ounce of carrot, one ounce of onions, and one ounce of salt pork sliced, half a teaspoonful of salt, quarter of a saltspoonful of pepper, three sprigs of parsley, one of thyme, three bay leaves, and six cloves; a gill of Spanish sauce or brown gravy is poured over it, and it is cooked in a moderate oven about an hour, until it is thoroughly done. The liver should be laid on a hot platter, while half a pint of Spanish sauce or gravy is stirred among the vegetables it was cooked with, and then strained over it. If served hot it is a most delicious and economical dish, being nearly as satisfactory to appetite as a heavy joint of roast meat.

54. **Blanquette of Veal.**—Cut three pounds of the breast of veal in pieces two inches square, put them in enough cold water to cover them, with one saltspoonful of white pepper, one teaspoonful of salt, a bouquet of sweet herbs, made as directed in Chapter first, and an onion stuck with three cloves; bring slowly to a boil, skim carefully until no more scum rises, and cook gently for thirty or forty minutes until the veal is tender; then drain it, returning the broth to the fire, and washing the meat in cold water; meantime make a white sauce by stirring together over the fire one ounce of butter and one ounce of flour, until they are smooth, then adding a pint and a half of the broth gradually, season with a little more salt and pepper if they are required, and with quarter of a saltspoonful of grated nutmeg; when the sauce has boiled up well, stir into it with an egg-whip the yolks of two

raw eggs, put in the meat, and cook for five minutes, stirring occasionally; a few mushrooms are a great improvement to the blanquette; or it may be served with two tablespoonfuls of chopped parsley sprinkled over it after it is put on a hot platter.

55. **Stuffed breast of Veal.**—Have the butcher make what is called a pocket in a three pound breast of veal, by cutting the flesh of the upper side free from the breast bones, taking care to leave three outer sides of the meat whole, so as to hold the stuffing; prepare a bed of vegetables, herbs, and pork, as directed for liver, in receipt No. 53; stuff the breast, sew it up, lay it on the vegetables, put four ounces of salt pork cut in thin slices on the top, season it with a teaspoonful of salt, and quarter of a saltspoonful of pepper, and bake it in a moderate oven about one hour, till thoroughly done; serve it with a brown gravy made the same as the liver gravy in receipt No. 53.

56. **Stuffing for Veal.**—Steep four ounces of bread in tepid water; chop one ounce of onion, and fry it yellow in one ounce of butter; wring the bread dry in a towel and add it to the butter and onion; season with one saltspoonful of salt, quarter of a saltspoonful each of pepper and powdered thyme, or mixed spices, and stir till scalding hot, then remove from the fire, stir in the yolk of one raw egg, and stuff the breast of veal with it. This is a very good stuffing for poultry, or lamb.

57. **Broiled Pork Cutlets.**—Make a Robert sauce, according to directions given below. Broil two pounds of cutlets from the neck of pork, being careful not to burn them, and dish them in a wreath on a hot platter with Robert sauce poured on the dish.

58. **Robert Sauce.**—Chop two ounces of onion, fry pale yellow with one ounce of butter, add two tablespoonfuls of spiced vinegar, and reduce one half by quick boiling; add half a pint of Spanish sauce, or brown gravy, and boil slowly for fifteen minutes; then season with a saltspoonful of salt, quarter of a saltspoonful of pepper, and two teaspoonfuls of French mustard, and serve.

59. **Pork Chops with Curry.**—First boil a quarter of a pound of rice according to receipt No. 60. Fry two pounds of pork chops cut from the loin, brown in a very little butter, pour off all the grease, add to them half a pint of Spanish sauce, and a tablespoonful of curry powder mixed smooth

with two tablespoonfuls of cold water; cover the sauce-pan, and simmer the chops for fifteen minutes; then dish them in a wreath on a hot platter, pour the sauce on the bottom of the dish, and fill the centre with rice.

60. **Boiled Rice.**—Wash a quarter of a pound of rice in plenty of cold water, put it into a quart of boiling water with a tablespoonful of salt, and boil it fast for twenty minutes; shake it out into a colander, drain it, and shake it from the colander into the centre of the dish of chops; do not stir it with a spoon.

61. **Broiled Pigs' Feet.**—Boil four well cleaned pickled pigs' feet in stock or boiling water with sweet herbs, until they are tender enough to permit the bones to come out readily; split them in halves, take out all the large bones; trim and shape them neatly, and cool them; when cold season them with pepper and salt, dip them first in melted butter and then in cracker dust, and broil them over a clear, moderate fire, turning them frequently; serve with a little melted butter, lemon juice, and chopped parsley over them.

62. **English Pork Pie.**—Make a plain pie crust by mixing together with the hand, half a pound of flour and quarter of a pound of butter, with enough cold water to make a stiff paste; roll out about six times on a well floured pastry board, folding the paste evenly each time; line the side of an earthen pie dish nearly to the bottom; in the bottom put a thin layer of bacon, about four ounces sliced; pare and slice half a quart of potatoes; chop two ounces of onion; cut two pounds of fresh lean pork in two-inch pieces; lay all these in the dish in layers, season with half a saltspoonful of pepper and the same quantity of powdered sage; fill the dish with any good cold gravy, cover with crust, wetting the edges to make them fit tight; ornament the surface according to your fancy, with leaves and fancy shapes cut out of the pastry; brush over with a raw egg beaten with a tablespoonful of water; bake in a moderate oven fifteen minutes; cover the top with paper, and bake one hour longer; serve hot, or cold, as desired.

63. **Fried Chicken, Spanish Style.**—Cut up a four pound chicken as for a *fricassee*, sprinkle the pieces with salt, and Spanish red pepper; put four ounces of lard in a frying pan on the fire, and when smoking hot, put in the legs, back, thighs, and wings; when they are half done, add the pieces of breast, two ounces of chopped onion, one clove of garlic chopped, a

bouquet of sweet herbs, made as directed in Chapter first, and fry seven minutes; add half a pound of raw ham cut in half inch dice, and fry till the chicken is tender; take it out and keep it hot, while you fry four large tomatoes cut in dice, and seasoned with salt and pepper to taste; then add the chicken, make it quite hot, and serve all together on a platter, like a *fricassee*.

64. **Chicken Fricassee.**—Cut a four pound tender chicken in joints, put it over the fire in enough cold water to cover it, with one dessertspoonful of salt, half a saltspoonful of pepper, a bouquet of sweet herbs, made as directed in Chapter first, two ounces of carrot, pared and left whole, and one dozen button onions peeled; skim frequently as often as any scum rises, simmer slowly until the chicken is tender, about an hour, and then take it up to keep hot while the sauce is made; strain out the vegetables, and set the broth to boil; mix one ounce of butter and one ounce of flour together over the fire until they become a smooth paste; then gradually add a pint and a half of the broth, stirring the sauce with an egg-whip until it is quite smooth, season it to taste with salt and pepper, and dish it on a hot platter; half a can of mushrooms greatly improve the flavor of the *fricassee*.

65. **Grilled Fowl.**—Cut the legs and second joints from two cold roast fowls; score them closely, season them with pepper and salt, and lay them by, ready to broil. Mince the rest of the meat fine. Make a white sauce by mixing together over the fire two ounces of butter and two of flour until they form a smooth paste; gradually add enough boiling milk to make a good thick sauce, season with half a teaspoonful of salt, quarter of a saltspoonful of white pepper, and the same quantity of grated nutmeg; add the minced fowl, and heat; now broil the legs and thighs, and after dishing the mince on a hot platter, lay them on it, and serve hot.

66. **Minced Chicken with Macaroni.**—Put four ounces of macaroni to blanch as directed in receipt No. 67. Cut two pounds of cold roast fowl in small slices, or scallops; and heat them in a white sauce, as directed in receipt No. 65: dish them in a border of macaroni, and serve hot.

67. **Macaroni with Cheese.**—Blanch four ounces of macaroni by putting it to boil in two quarts of boiling water and a tablespoonful of salt; boil it until it is tender enough to pierce with the finger nail, drain it in a colander, wash

it well in cold water, and let it remain in water while you prepare a white sauce of one ounce of butter, one of flour, and boiling milk, as directed in receipt No. 65:—put the macaroni into it with two ounces of grated cheese, Parmesan is the best; heat it thoroughly; dish it in a border around the minced fowl, which should be piled in the middle of the dish.

68. **Broiled Pigeons.**—Carefully pluck and draw eight pigeons, split them down the middle of the back, flatten them by pounding them with the blade of a heavy knife, broil them on a greased gridiron, the inside first; lay each one on a slice of buttered toast, and dress them with a little *maître d'hotel* butter, made according to receipt No. 16.

69. **Salmi of Duck.**—Cut two cold roast wild ducks in joints; put them into a sauce-pan with enough Spanish sauce to cover them, and add two dozen olives with the stones removed; season to taste with salt and pepper, being guided in this by the seasoning of the Spanish sauce; heat thoroughly; meantime cut a dozen heart shaped *croutons*, or slices of bread about two inches long and one wide, and fry them brown in plenty of hot fat; when the *salmi* is hot, pour it on a hot dish, and arrange the *croutons* around the border; serve hot.

70. **Civet of Hare.**—Skin a pair of leverets, or young hares, carefully wipe them outside with a damp cloth; remove the entrails, and wash the interior with a cup of vinegar, which must be saved; cut them into joints as you would divide a chicken for *fricassee*; cut the back and loins in pieces about two inches square; peel two dozen button onions, and fry them light brown in two ounces of butter, with half a pound of lean ham cut in half inch dice; add the hare, and brown well; stir in two ounces of dry flour, add three gills of broth, and one gill of the vinegar used to wash the hare, or two gills of claret, season with one teaspoonful of salt, one saltspoonful of ground cloves, and half a saltspoonful of pepper; simmer gently about one hour, until the hare is tender, and serve on a hot platter like chicken *fricassee*.

71. **Jugged Hare.**—Prepare two hares as for a *civet*, in receipt No. 70; in the cup of vinegar and half a pint of Spanish sauce, (or in their place one pint of claret,) put the yellow rind of one lemon, a bouquet of sweet herbs, prepared as in Chapter first, eight cloves, two blades of mace, two inches of stick cinnamon, eight allspice, one ounce of onion whole, one ounce of

carrot whole; boil all these together half an hour when you are preparing the hare, as in receipt No. 70; lay the browned pieces of hare in an earthen jar; season them a little with a teaspoonful of salt, and quarter of a saltspoonful of pepper; strain the gravy made as above into the jar; put on the cover; fasten it in place with a paste made of flour and water, and oiled on the top to prevent cracking. Bake the hare in a moderate oven three hours. When you are nearly ready to dish it, cut a slice of bread two inches thick, the entire side of a large loaf, trim it to a perfect oval, fry it light brown in hot fat, put it on a platter, arrange the hare on it, and pour the gravy over; serve hot.

72. **Stuffed Eggs.**—Boil eight eggs for ten minutes, until quite hard, lay them in cold water until they are quite cold; make a white sauce, as directed in receipt No. 65; soak two ounces of stale bread in tepid water for five minutes, and wring it dry in a towel; put one ounce of grated cheese, Parmesan is the best, in a sauce-pan with one saltspoonful of salt, half that quantity of white pepper, as much cayenne as can be taken up on the point of a very small pen-knife blade, a teaspoonful of lemon juice, two ounces of butter, and a gill of the white sauce; cut the eggs carefully in halves lengthwise after removing the shells, rub the yolks through a sieve with a silver spoon, and add them with the bread to the sauce, as prepared above; stir these ingredients over the fire until they cleave from the sides of the sauce-pan, when they will be scalding hot; on a hot platter put a layer of the white sauce as a foundation for the eggs; fill the whites with the forcemeat, rounding it up to look like the entire yolk of an egg, set them on a dish in a pyramid, and heat them in a moderate oven; send whatever white sauce you have left to the table in a boat, with the dish of eggs.

When, after preparing the eggs for the oven, they are sprinkled with grated cheese, and cracker dust, and then browned, they are called gratinated eggs, or stuffed eggs, *au gratin*, and are served without any sauce.

73. **How to make Omelettes.**—There is no great difficulty in making omelettes, and as they may be expeditiously prepared and served they are a convenient resource when an extra dish is required at short notice; care should be taken to beat the eggs only until they are light, to put the omelette into a well heated and buttered pan, and *never to turn it in the pan*, as this flattens and toughens it; if the pan be large, and only three or four eggs be

used in making the omelette, the pan should be tipped and held by the handle so that the eggs will cook in a small space upon one side of it; instead of spreading all over it, and becoming too dry in the process of cooking.

There are three secrets in the making of a good omelette, namely, the separate beating of the eggs, the knack of stirring it upon the fire, and the method of transferring it from the fire to the table. If you will carefully follow the directions here given, you can produce a dish dainty enough to satisfy the most fastidious eater.

74. **Plain Omelette.**—If you have to serve eight persons, make three omelettes as follows:

Put one half an ounce (about a tablespoonful) of butter into a clean, smooth frying-pan, and set it upon the back of the stove to melt; stir the yolks of three eggs with a saltspoonful of salt for one minute; beat the whites of three eggs to a stiff froth with an egg-whip, beginning slowly, and gradually increasing the speed until the froth will not leave the dish if it be turned bottom up; this will take from three to five minutes, according to the freshness of the eggs; now pour the yolks into the froth, and mix them gently with a silver spoon, turning the bowl of the spoon over and over, but do not stir in a circle, or rapidly; put the frying-pan containing the melted butter over the fire, pour in the omelette, and stir it with a large two-pronged fork (a carving fork will do), carefully raising the edges with the fork as fast as they cook, and turning them toward the centre, until the omelette lies in the middle of the pan in a light mass, cooked soft or hard to suit the taste; when done to the desired degree, turn it out upon a hot dish *without touching it with either fork or spoon*, and send it to the table immediately. Another excellent method is to beat three eggs, without separating the whites and yolks, with one tablespoonful of milk, and a little salt and pepper, and put them into a frying-pan containing two ounces of butter browned; let the omelette stand for a moment, and then turn the edges up gently with a fork, and shake the pan to prevent it burning or sticking at the bottom; five minutes will fry it a delicate brown, and it should then be doubled and sent to the table at once on a hot dish. Three eggs will make an omelette large enough for two persons, if any other dish is to be served with it. There are several varieties of omelettes, each named after the ingredient prominent in the composition. We subjoin some excellent receipts, which may be based upon the first-mentioned method of preparation and cooking.

75. **Omelette with Herbs.**—Stir into the yolks of three eggs a saltspoonful of salt, half a teaspoonful of chopped parsley, one tablespoonful of chopped mushrooms, and one tablespoonful of shallot or white onion; beat the whites of three eggs to a stiff froth, add them to the yolks, and cook as in the first receipt.

76. **Omelette with Ham, Tongue, or Cheese.**—Use chopped or grated ham, or tongue, or cheese, in the proportion of one tablespoonful to one egg; proceed to mix and cook in the same way as for omelette with herbs.

77. **Omelette with Oysters.**—Blanch one dozen small Blue Point oysters, by bringing them just to a boil in their own liquor, seasoned with a dust of cayenne, a saltspoonful of salt, and a grate of nutmeg; mix an omelette as above, omitting the herbs, place it over the fire, and when it begins to cook at the edges, place the oysters, without any liquor, in its centre, and fold and serve it in the same manner as the omelette with herbs.

78. **Omelette with Mushrooms.**—Choose a dozen small, even sized mushrooms; if they are canned, simply warm them in the essence in which they are preserved, and if they are fresh, peel them by dipping them, held by the stem, into boiling water for one moment, and heat them over the fire with half an ounce of butter and half a saltspoonful of salt put over them; prepare the omelette as above, and as soon as the edges begin to cook, place the mushrooms in the centre, and fold and serve like the omelette with herbs.

79. **Spanish Omelette.**—Peel two large ripe tomatoes, cut them in thin slices, put them into a frying pan with an ounce of butter, a saltspoonful of salt, and a dust of pepper, and toss them to prevent burning, until they are just cooked through; make an omelette as above, and as soon as its edges are cooked put in the tomatoes, and fold and serve the same as the omelette with herbs.

80. **Oriental Omelette.**—Heat a thick earthen plate over a charcoal or wood fire, until it will melt butter enough to cover the bottom of it, dust on

the butter a little pepper, and sprinkle on a little salt; break into it as many eggs as will lay upon it without crowding, and brown them underneath; then set them where the heat of the fire will strike their tops, and let them color a pale yellow; salt them a little, and serve them very hot upon the same dish upon which they were cooked.

81. **Omelette with Preserves.**—Prepare an omelette as directed in receipt No. 77, substituting any kind of jelly or preserves for the oysters.

82. **How to Cook Macaroni.**—This is one of the most wholesome and economical of foods, and can be varied so as to give a succession of palatable dishes at a very small cost. The imported macaroni can be bought at Italian stores for about fifteen cents a pound; and that quantity when boiled yields nearly three times its bulk, if it has been manufactured for any length of time. In cooking it is generally combined with meat gravy, tomato sauce, and cheese; Gruyere and Parmesan cheese, which are the kinds most used by foreign cooks, can be readily obtained at any large grocery, the price of the former being about thirty-five cents per pound, and the latter varying from forty to eighty cents, according to the commercial spirit of the vendor; the trade price quoted on grocers' trade lists being thirty-eight cents per pound, for prime quality. This cheese is of a greenish color, a little salt in taste and flavored with delicate herbs; the nearest domestic variety is sage-cheese, which may be used when Parmesan can not be obtained. If in heating Parmesan cheese it appears oily, it is from the lack of moisture, and this can be supplied by adding a few tablespoonfuls of broth, and stirring it over the fire for a minute. When more macaroni has been boiled than is used, it can be kept perfectly good by laying it in fresh water, which must be changed every day. There are several forms of Italian paste, but the composition is almost identical, all being made from the interior part of the finest wheat grown on the Mediterranean shores: the largest tubes, about the size of a lead pencil, are called *macaroni*; the second variety, as large as a common pipe-stem, is termed *mazzini*; and the smallest is *spaghetti*, or threads; *vermicelli* comes to market in the form of small coils or hanks of fine yellowish threads; and *Italian paste* appears in small letters, and various fanciful shapes. Macaroni is generally known as a rather luxurious dish among the wealthy; but it should become one of the chief foods of the people, for it contains more gluten, or the nutritious portion of wheat, than bread.

83. **Macaroni with Béchamel Sauce.**—Heat three quarts of water, containing three tablespoonfuls of salt, to the boiling point; boil half a pound of *macaroni* in it until it is tender enough to pierce easily with the finger nail; then drain it in a colander, and wash it well in cold water; while it is boiling make a *Béchamel*, or white sauce, as in receipt No. 84: put just enough of it with the *macaroni* to moisten it, heat it thoroughly; shake it up well with two forks to make the cheese fibrous, put it on a hot dish, sprinkle with half an ounce of grated Parmesan cheese, and serve it hot.

84. **Béchamel Sauce, with Parmesan Cheese.**—Stir together over the fire two ounces of butter, and two ounces of flour, until they are perfectly blended, boiling one pint of milk meantime; when the butter and flour are smooth, pour the boiling milk into them, stir in two ounces of grated Parmesan gradually and melt it thoroughly, stirring constantly until the sauce is smooth; if cream is used instead of milk, and the Parmesan cheese omitted, the same is called *Cream Béchamel*.

85. **Macaroni Milanaise style.**—Have ready some tomato sauce, made according to receipt No. 52, or use some fresh tomatoes passed through a sieve with a wooden spoon, and highly seasoned; and two ounces of grated Parmesan cheese; put half a pound of imported Italian *macaroni* in three quarts of boiling water, with two tablespoonfuls of salt, one saltspoonful of pepper in coarse pieces, called *mignonette* pepper, and a teaspoonful of butter; boil rapidly for about twenty minutes, or until you can easily pierce it with the finger nail, then drain it in a colander, run plenty of cold water from the faucet through it, and lay it in a pan of cold water until you are ready to use it. Put into a sauce-pan one gill of tomato sauce, one ounce of butter, and one gill of Spanish sauce, or any rich meat gravy free from fat, and stir until they are smoothly blended: put a half inch layer of *macaroni* on the bottom of a dish, moisten it with four tablespoonfuls of the sauce, sprinkle over it half an ounce of the grated cheese; make three other layers like this, using all the *macaroni*, cheese, and sauce, and brown the *macaroni* in a hot oven for about five minutes; serve it hot.

86. **Macaroni with Tomato Sauce.**—Boil half a pound of *spaghetti* or *macaroni* as directed in receipt No. 83, and lay it in cold water. Make a tomato sauce as follows, and dress the *macaroni* with it, using only enough

to moisten it, and sprinkling the top with half an ounce of grated cheese; serve it hot.

87. **Tomato Sauce.**—Boil together, for one hour, half a can of tomatoes, or six large, fresh ones, one gill of broth of any kind, one sprig of thyme, one sprig of parsley, three whole cloves, three peppercorns, and half an ounce of onion sliced; rub them through a sieve with a wooden spoon, and set the sauce to keep hot; mix together over the fire one ounce of butter, and half an ounce of flour, and when smooth, incorporate with the tomato sauce.

88. **Timbale of Macaroni.** (*A sweet dish.*)—Boil half a pound of *macaroni* of the largest size, in boiling water and salt for fifteen minutes; drain it in a colander, wash it well, lay by one quarter of it, and put the rest into a sauce-pan with one ounce of butter, one pint of milk or cream, four ounces of sugar, one teaspoonful of vanilla flavoring, and a saltspoonful of salt; simmer it gently while you line a well buttered three pint plain mould with the best pieces you have reserved, coiling them regularly in the bottom and up the sides of the mould; put what you do not use among that in the sauce-pan, and as soon as it is tender fill the mould with it, and set it in a hot oven for fifteen minutes; then turn it out on a dish, dust it with powdered sugar, and serve it hot, with a pudding sauce.

89. **Vanilla Cream Sauce.**—Put three ounces of powdered sugar into a sauce-pan with one ounce of corn starch, and one gill of cold water; mix them smooth off the fire; then put the sauce-pan on the fire and pour in half a pint of boiling milk, stirring smooth with an egg-whip for about ten minutes, when the sauce will be thoroughly cooked; flavor it with one teaspoonful of vanilla, and serve with pudding at once.

CHAPTER VI.

LARGE ROASTS.

Since roast or rather baked meats so often play the chief part in American dinners, a few directions will be useful in connection with their cooking. The object in cooking meat is to prepare it for easy mastication and complete digestion; and it should be accomplished with the least possible waste of the valuable juices of the meat. The roasting of meat before the fire is not often possible in ordinary kitchens, but with a well managed oven the same result can be attained. If meat is placed before a slow fire, or in a cool oven, the little heat that reaches it serves only to draw out its juices, and with them its nutritious elements. The albumen of its cut surfaces coagulates at the temperature of a bright, clear fire, or a hot oven, and thus seals up the juices so that only a part of them escape, and those are collected in the form of a rich brown, highly flavored crust, upon the surface of well roasted meat. A good temperature for baking meat is from 320° to 400° Fahr. If the meat is put into a very hot oven for a few moments to harden the outside, the heat can subsequently be moderated, and the cooking finished more slowly, so that the meat will be sufficiently well done, but not burned. Meats should be roasted about twenty minutes to a pound, to be moderately well done; the fire should be clear, and steady, in order that an equal heat may reach the joint and keep its interior steam at the proper degree of heat; after the right length of time has elapsed, care being taken meantime that the meat does not burn, it may be tested by pressing it with the fingers; if it is rare it will spring back when the pressure is removed; if it is moderately well done the resistance to pressure will be very slight; and if it is thoroughly cooked it will remain heavy under the fingers; never test it by cutting into it with a knife, or puncturing it with a fork, for in this way you waste the rich juices. If you wish to froth roast meat, dredge a little flour over its surface, and brown it a few moments before serving it. If it is to be glazed, brush it with clear stock concentrated to a paste by rapid boiling, or dust a little powdered sugar over it, and in both cases return it to the oven to set the glaze.

90. **Roast Beef with Yorkshire Pudding.**—Have three ribs of prime beef prepared by the butcher for roasting, all the bones being taken out if it is desirable to carve a clean slice off the top; secure it in place with stout twine; do not use skewers, as the unnecessary holes they make permit the meat-juices to escape; lay it in the dripping pan on a bed of the following vegetables, cut in small pieces; one small onion, half a carrot, half a turnip, three sprigs of parsley, one sprig of thyme, and three bay leaves; *do not put any water in the dripping pan*; its temperature can not rise to a degree equal in heat to that of the fat outside of the beef, and can not assist in its cooking, but serves only to lower the temperature of the meat, where it touches it, and consequently to soften the surface and extract the juices; *do not season it until the surface is partly carbonized by the heat*, as salt applied to the cut fibre draws out their juices. If you use a roasting oven before the fire, the meat should be similarly prepared by tying in place, and it should be put on the spit carefully; sufficient drippings for basting will flow from it, and it should be seasoned when half done; when entirely done, which will be in fifteen minutes to each pound of meat, the joint should be kept hot until served, but should be served as soon as possible to be good. When gravy is made, half a pint of hot water should be added to the dripping pan, after the vegetables have been removed, and the gravy should be boiled briskly for a few minutes, until it is thick enough, and seasoned to suit the palate of the family; some persons thicken it with a teaspoonful of flour, which should be mixed with two tablespoonfuls of cold water before it is stirred into the gravy.

91. **Yorkshire Pudding.**—Put seven ounces of flour into a bowl with one teaspoonful of salt; mix it smoothly with enough milk, say half a pint, to make a smooth, stiff batter; then gradually add enough more milk to amount in all to one pint and a half, and three eggs well beaten; mix it thoroughly with an egg-whip, pour it into a well buttered baking pan, bake it in the oven one hour and a half, if it is to be served with baked beef; or if it is to accompany beef roasted before the fire, one hour in the oven, and then half an hour under the meat on the spit, to catch the gravy which flows from the joint. To serve it cut it into pieces two or three inches square before taking it from the pan, and send it to the table on a hot dish covered with a napkin, with the roast beef.

92. **Roast Loin of Veal.**—Take out the chine, or back-bone, from a loin of veal weighing about six pounds, being careful to leave the piece of meat as whole as possible; chop up the bones and put them in a dripping pan with two ounces of carrot, one ounce of turnip, and quarter of an ounce of parsley; stuff the veal with a forcemeat made as in receipt No. 93, roll it up neatly, tie it firmly with stout cord, lay it on the vegetables in the pan, and roast it one hour and a half. When done take it from the pan, and keep it hot while you prepare the gravy by putting half a pint of hot water in the pan, boiling it up once, and straining it; or if desirable thicken it with a teaspoonful of flour smoothly dissolved in two tablespoonfuls of cold water and stirred with the gravy.

93. **Stuffing for Veal.**—Cut two ounces of salt pork in quarter inch dice, and fry it brown in half an ounce of butter, with one ounce of chopped onion; while these ingredients are frying, soak eight ounces of stale bread in tepid water, and then wring it dry in a napkin; add it to the onion when it is brown, with one tablespoonful of chopped parsley, half a saltspoonful of powdered thyme, and the same quantity of dried and powdered celery, and white pepper, and one teaspoonful of salt; mix all these over the fire until they are scalding hot, and cleave from the pan; then stir in one raw egg, and use it with the veal.

94. **Roast Lamb with Mint Sauce.**—Choose a plump, fat fore-quarter of lamb, which is quite as finely flavored and less expensive than the hind-quarter; secure it in shape with stout cord, lay it in a dripping pan with one sprig of parsley, three sprigs of mint, and one ounce of carrot sliced; put it into a quick oven, and roast it fifteen minutes to each pound; when half done season it with salt and pepper, and baste it occasionally with the drippings flowing from it. When done serve it with a gravy-boat full of mint sauce.

95. **Mint Sauce cold.**—Melt four ounces of brown sugar in a sauce boat with half a pint of vinegar, add three tablespoonfuls of chopped mint, and serve cold with roast lamb.

96. **Hot Mint Sauce.**—Put one pint of vinegar into a sauce-pan with four ounces of white sugar, and reduce by rapid boiling to half a pint, stirring to

prevent burning; add a gill of cold water, and boil for five minutes; then add three tablespoonfuls of chopped mint, and serve with lamb.

97. **Roast Pork with Apple Sauce.**—Neatly trim a loin of fresh pork weighing about six pounds; put it into a dripping pan on three bay leaves, quarter of an ounce of parsley, one ounce of onion, and the same quantity of carrot sliced, and roast it about twenty minutes to each pound; when half done, season it with salt and pepper; when brown, serve it with a border of Parisian potatoes, prepared according to receipt No. 2, and send it to the table with a bowl of apple sauce.

98. **Apple Sauce.**—Pare and slice one quart of good tart apples; put them into a sauce-pan with half a pint of cold water; stir them often enough to prevent burning, and simmer them until tender, about twenty minutes will be long enough; then rub them through a sieve with a wooden spoon, add a saltspoonful of powdered cloves, and four ounces of sugar, or less according to the taste; serve in a bowl, with the roast pork.

99. **Roast Turkey with Cranberry Sauce.**—Choose a fat tender turkey weighing about six or seven pounds; pluck it, carefully remove the pin-feathers, singe the bird over the flame of an alcohol lamp, or a few drops of alcohol poured on a plate and lighted; wipe it with a damp towel and see that it is properly drawn by slitting the skin at the back of the neck, and taking out the crop without tearing the skin of the breast; loosen the heart, liver, and lungs, by introducing the fore-finger at the neck, and then draw them, with the entrails, from the vent. Unless you have broken the gall, or the entrails, in drawing the bird *do not wash it*, for this greatly impairs the flavor, and partly destroys the nourishing qualities of the flesh. Twist the tips of the wings back under the shoulders, stuff the bird with forcemeat made according to receipt No. 100; bend the legs as far up toward the breast as possible, secure the thigh bones in that position by a trussing cord or skewer; then bring the legs down, and fasten them close to the vent. Pound the breast bone down, first laying a towel over it. Lay a thin slice of salt pork over the breast to baste it until sufficient drippings run from the bird; baste it frequently, browning it on all sides by turning it about in the pan; use a clean towel to turn it with, *but do not run a fork into it or you will waste its juices*: when it is half done season it with two teaspoonfuls of salt and one saltspoonful of powdered herbs, made according to directions in

Chapter first; when it has cooked about twenty minutes to each pound, dish it, and keep it hot while you make a gravy by adding half a pint of water to the drippings in the pan, first taking off a little of the superfluous fat, and thickening it if desired with a teaspoonful of flour mixed with two tablespoonfuls of cold water; serve the turkey hot with a gravy-boat full of gravy and a dish of cranberry sauce made according to receipt No. 101. The same directions for drawing, trussing, and roasting will apply to other poultry and game.

100. **Forcemeat for Roast Poultry.**—Steep eight ounces of stale bread in tepid water for five minutes, and wring it dry in a clean towel; meantime chop fine four ounces each of fresh veal and pork, or use instead, eight ounces of good sausage meat; grate eight ounces of good rather dry cheese; fry one ounce of onion in one ounce of butter to a light yellow color; add the bread, meat, and cheese, season with a saltspoonful of powdered herbs, made according to directions in Chapter first, a teaspoonful of salt, a saltspoonful of pepper, and two whole eggs; mix well and use.

101. **Cranberry Sauce.**—Carefully pick and wash one quart of cranberries; put them over the fire in a sauce-pan with half a pint of cold water; bring them to a boil, and boil them gently for fifteen minutes, stirring them occasionally to prevent burning; then add four ounces of white sugar, and boil them slowly until they are soft enough to pass through a sieve with a wooden spoon; the sauce is then ready to serve.

102. **Roast Chicken with Duchesse Potatoes.**—Prepare and roast a pair of chickens as directed in receipt No. 99; or for the stuffing named in that receipt substitute No. 93; meantime boil one quart of potatoes, for mashing, and make twelve heart-shaped *croutons* or pieces of bread fried in hot fat: lay the Duchesse potatoes around the chickens when it is dished, and the *croutons* in an outer circle, with the points outward.

103. **Duchesse Potatoes.**—Mash one quart of hot boiled potatoes through a fine colander with the potato masher; mix with them one ounce of butter, one level teaspoonful of salt, half a saltspoonful of white pepper, quarter of a saltspoonful of grated nutmeg, and the yolks of two raw eggs; pour the potato out on a plate, and then form it with a knife into small cakes, two inches long and one inch wide; lay them on a buttered tin, brush them over

the top with an egg beaten up with a teaspoonful of cold water, and color them golden brown in a moderate oven.

104. **Roast Duck with Watercresses.**—Prepare and roast a pair of ducks as directed in receipt No. 99, and serve them with a border of a few watercresses, and a salad bowl containing the rest of a quart, prepared as in receipt No. 105.

105. **Romaine Sauce for Watercresses.**—Grate half an ounce of onion, and use two tablespoonfuls of vinegar to wash it off the grater; to these add a saltspoonful of sugar, a tablespoonful of lemon juice, three tablespoonfuls of olive oil, six capers chopped fine, as much cayenne as can be taken up on the point of a very small pen-knife blade, a level saltspoonful of salt, and quarter of a saltspoonful of pepper; mix well, and use for dressing watercresses, or any other green salad. A few cold boiled potatoes sliced and mixed with this dressing, and a head of lettuce, makes a very nice potato salad.

106. **Roast Goose with Onion Sauce.**—Prepare a goose as directed in receipt No. 99; stuff it with onion stuffing made according to receipt No. 107; serve it with a gravy boat full of onion sauce made according to receipt No. 108.

107. **Sage and Onion Stuffing.**—Pare six ounces of onion, and bring them to a boil in three different waters; soak eight ounces of stale bread in tepid water, and wring it dry in a towel; scald ten sage leaves; when the onions are tender, which will be in about half an hour, chop them with the sage leaves, add them to the bread, with one ounce of butter, the yolks of two raw eggs, one level teaspoonful of salt, and half a saltspoonful of pepper; mix and use.

108. **Onion Sauce.**—Prepare six ounces of onions as in receipt No. 107; chop them fine, pass them through a sieve with a wooden spoon, and put them into half a pint of boiling milk, with one ounce of butter, one saltspoonful of salt, and one quarter of a saltspoonful of pepper.

109. **Roast Wild Duck.**—Prepare a pair of ducks as directed in receipt No. 99; do not stuff them, but tie over the breasts slices of pork or bacon; roast

fifteen minutes to the pound; serve with gravy in a boat and quarters of lemon on the same dish.

110. **Roast Partridge.**—Prepare a pair of partridges as in receipt No. 99, but do not stuff them; tie over the breasts slices of pork or bacon, and roast about twenty-five minutes; serve with bread sauce.

111. **Bread Sauce.**—Peel and slice an onion weighing full an ounce, simmer it half an hour in one pint of milk, strain it, and to the milk add two ounces of stale bread, broken in small pieces, one ounce of butter, one saltspoonful of salt, and quarter of a saltspoonful of nutmeg and pepper mixed; strain, passing through a sieve with a spoon, and serve hot.

CHAPTER VII.

BOILED DISHES.

Boiling is the most economical way of cooking, if properly done; there are several important points to be considered in this connection. We have already said that the best method of cooking meat is that which preserves all its nourishing juices; if in addition to this we can prepare it in such a way as to present a large available surface to the action of the digestive juices, we would seem to have reached culinary perfection. Judicious boiling accomplishes this: and we cannot do better than to follow Liebig's plan to first plunge the meat into boiling water, and boil it five minutes to coagulate the albumen to a sufficient depth to form a crust upon the surface, and thus confine the juices, and then add enough cold water to reduce the temperature to 158° Fahr., if the meat is to be rare, or to 165° Fahr., if it is to be well done; and to maintain this gentle heat until the meat is tender. There is comparatively little waste in boiling, from the fact that fat melts less quickly than in broiling or roasting, and the covering of the pot retards evaporation, while the water absorbed by the meat adds to its bulk to a certain extent without detracting from its quality. A strainer or plate should be placed in the bottom of the pot to prevent burning; the pot should be skimmed clear as soon as it boils, and the subsequent simmering should be gentle and steady; there should always be sufficient water to cover the meat in order to keep it plump. Less body of heat is required to boil in copper or iron pots, than in those made of tin, especially if the latter have polished surfaces which throw off the heat. The pot-liquor from boiled meat should always be strained into an earthen jar and left to cool; the fat can then be taken off for kitchen use, and the liquor utilized as the basis for some kind of soup.

112. **Leg of Mutton with Caper Sauce.**—Put a leg of mutton, weighing about six pounds, on the fire in enough boiling hot water to cover it; boil it for five minutes, skimming it as often as any scum rises, then pour in enough cold water to reduce the heat to about 160° Fahr., season with a tablespoonful of salt, and simmer the meat at that heat until it is tender,

allowing about twenty minutes cooking to each pound of meat; if turnips are to be served with it as a garnish, choose them of equal size, pare them smoothly, and boil them with the mutton; if the vegetables are cooked first take them up without breaking, and set them back off the fire, in a little of the mutton stock, to keep hot. Just before dishing the meat, make a caper sauce, as directed in receipt No. 113; serve the mutton on a hot dish, with the turnips laid around it, and send the sauce in a gravy-boat to the table with it.

113. **Caper Sauce.**—Put one ounce of butter and one ounce of flour in a sauce-pan over the fire, and stir until smoothly melted; gradually pour in half a pint of boiling water, season with one teaspoonful of salt, and quarter of a saltspoonful of white pepper, and stir until the sauce coats the spoon when you lift it out; take it from the fire, and stir in two ounces of butter, and two tablespoonfuls of small capers, and serve at once. *Do not permit the sauce to boil after you have added the butter, as it may turn rancid.*

114. **Boiled Ham with Madeira Sauce.**—Choose a ham by running a thin bladed knife close to the bone, and if the odor which follows the cut is sweet the ham is good; soak it in cold water for twenty-four hours, changing the water once; scrape it well, and trim off any ragged parts; put it in enough cold water to cover it, with an onion weighing about one ounce, stuck with six cloves, and a bouquet made according to directions in Chapter first, and boil it four hours. Take it from the fire and let it cool in the pot-liquor. Then take it up carefully, remove the skin, dust it with sifted bread or cracker crumbs, and brown it in the oven. Serve it either hot or cold; if hot send it to the table with a gravy boat full of Madeira sauce.

115. **Madeira Sauce.**—Put over the fire in a thick sauce-pan one pint of Spanish sauce made according to receipt No. 44, or the same quantity of any rich brown gravy, season with salt and pepper to taste; the seasoning must depend on the flavor of the gravy; when scalding hot add half a pint of Madeira wine, and stir till the sauce is thick enough to coat the spoon; then strain through a fine sieve, and serve hot.

116. **Beef á la Mode Jardiniere.**—Daube a seven pound piece of round of beef, by inserting, with the grain, pieces of larding pork, cut as long as the meat is thick, and about half an inch square, setting the strips of pork about

two inches apart; this can be done either with a large larding needle, called a *sonde*, or by first making a hole with the carving-knife steel, and then thrusting the pork in with the fingers; lay the beef in a deep bowl containing the *marinade*, or pickle, given in receipt No. 117, and let it stand from two to ten days in a cool place, turning it over every day. Then put it into a deep pot just large enough to hold it, together with the *marinade*, and turn it occasionally over the fire until it is nicely browned; cover it with hot stock or water, and simmer it gently four hours. When it has been cooking three hours cut about four ounces each of carrots and turnips in the shape of olives; pare two dozen button onions; and cut one pint of string beans in pieces one inch long; put all these vegetables on the fire in cold water, in separate vessels, each containing a teaspoonful of salt, and half a saltspoonful of sugar, and let them boil till tender; then lay them in cold water to keep them white, until ready to use them. When the meat is tender, take it up, and keep it warm; strain the sauce in which it has cooked, and stir it over the fire until it is thick enough to coat the spoon; drain the vegetables, and let them scald up in the sauce, and pour all over the beef.

117. **Marinade.**—Cut in slices, four ounces each of carrot and onion, two ounces of turnip, and one ounce of leeks; chop a quarter of an ounce each of parsley and celery, if in season; slice one lemon; add to these one level tablespoonful of salt, one saltspoonful of pepper, six cloves, four allspice, one inch of stick cinnamon, two blades of mace, one gill of oil and one of vinegar, half a pint of red wine, and one pint of water. Mix all these ingredients thoroughly, and use the *marinade* for beef, game, or poultry, always keeping it in a cool place.

118. **Boiled Fowl with Oyster Sauce.**—Prepare a pair of fowls in accordance with receipt No. 99, but do not stuff them; put them into boiling water enough to cover them, with a level tablespoonful of salt to each quart of water; skim until clear, and boil slowly until tender, about fifteen minutes to a pound; when nearly done, make an oyster sauce, as directed in receipt No. 119, and serve it on the same dish with the fowls, sprinkling them with a teaspoonful of chopped parsley.

119. **Oyster Sauce.**—Blanch one quart of oysters by bringing them to a boil in their own liquor; drain them, saving the liquor; wash them in cold water, and set them away from the fire until you are ready to use them; stir

one ounce of butter and one ounce of flour together over the fire until they form a smooth paste, strain into them enough of the oyster liquor and that the chicken was boiled in to make a sauce as thick as melted butter; season with a teaspoonful of salt, quarter of a saltspoonful of white pepper, and the same of grated nutmeg; put in the oysters, and serve.

CHAPTER VIII.

SALADS AND SALAD SAUCES.

"The very herbs of the field yield nourishment, and bread and water make a feast for a temperate man," says Plato; and indeed the healthfulness of fresh vegetables is well enough known in our day; we include under this term not only the edible roots, but the young shoots of succulent plants, rich in nitrates and mineral salts, which play an important part in the preparation of salads. Americans are beginning to realize the wealth of green food abounding in their gardens and fields, which they have too long abandoned to their beasts of burden. We are wise in letting the ox eat grass for us, but with the grass he too often consumes tender herbs which might find a place on our own tables, to the advantage of appetite and digestion. Dandelion, corn-salad, chicory, mint, sorrel, fennel, marshmallows, tarragon, chives, mustard, and cresses, and their numerous kind, grow wild, or can be cultivated with but little trouble; and should find their way to favor in every family, for with the oil and vinegar employed in dressing them, they promote digestion, and purify the system; while the condiments used with them are of decided medicinal value.

There is some degree of truth in the idea that a salad-maker is born, not made, and yet with due care and delicate manipulation, almost any deft-handed and neat-minded individual may become an expert salad dresser. Most careful preparation of the green vegetables is imperatively necessary to the production of a good salad; they must be freshened in cool water, cleaned of all foreign matter, well drained upon a clean napkin; and, above all, torn with the fingers, and not cut with a knife. Then the various ingredients should be very delicately and deliberately compounded, and withal by a quick and cunning hand, and the result will be perfection. Below we give the receipts for a class of salads best adapted for general use.

In the preparation of all salads only good oil should be used, as none other will produce invariably satisfactory results. The very best salads are often the result of the inspiration of the moment, when the necessity arises for substituting some ingredient near at hand for one not to be obtained, as in the case of the shad-roe salad mentioned below. The formula called for Russian caviare, but Russian caviare was not to be had, and a cold shad-roe was; the consequence was its substitution and the alteration of one or two other ingredients, and the result, we do not hesitate to say, was the production of one of the most delicious salads ever invented. Let careful housekeepers not given to these "foreign dishes" remember that they are not only appetizing but economical.

120. **Spring Salad.**—Break one pint of fresh mustard tops, and one of cresses, tear one good-sized lettuce, and chop two green onions; place all lightly in a dish, and ornament it with celery and slices of boiled beet. Use it with a cream dressing.

121. **Watercress Salad.**—Serve one quart of watercresses with one chopped green onion, one teaspoonful of ground horseradish, one tablespoonful of lemon juice, and two of oil, simply poured over.

122. **Mint Salad.**—Wash and clean the tender tops of one quart of spearmint, lay them in a bowl with one tablespoonful of chopped chives, and dress them with brown sugar and vinegar, or *sweet sauce*. This is an excellent accompaniment for roast lamb.

123. **Cauliflower Salad.**—Place in a salad bowl one underdone cauliflower, broken in branches, six small silver onions, six radishes, ornament with the hearts of two white lettuces, and one dessertspoonful each of chopped olives and capers; dress it with cream sauce, or plain oil and vinegar.

124. **Dandelion Salad.**—This salad is a favorite European dish; one pint of the plants are carefully washed and placed in a salad bowl with an equal quantity of watercresses, three green onions or leeks sliced, a teaspoonful of salt, and plenty of oil or cream dressing. This is one of the most healthful and refreshing of all early salads.

125. **Asparagus Salad.**—Cut the green tops of two bunches of cold asparagus one inch long, mix them with the leaves of one lettuce, a few

sprigs of mint, and a teaspoonful of powdered sugar, ornament with tufts of leaves, and serve with a Mayonnaise.

126. **Shad-roe Salad.**—Boil two roes, separate the grains by washing them in vinegar, place them in a salad bowl, with one head of tender lettuce and one pint of ripe tomatoes cut thin; dress them with two tablespoonfuls each of oil, lemon juice, and strained tomato pulp, seasoned with cayenne pepper.

127. **Green Pea Salad.**—Place one pint of cold boiled peas in a bowl with one tablespoonful of powdered sugar; pour over them two tablespoonfuls of oil and one of vinegar, and garnish with two cucumbers delicately sliced. This salad is excellent with a Mayonnaise.

128. **Orange Salad.**—Divest four under-ripe oranges of all rind and pith, slice them into a dish, season with a little cayenne pepper, add the rind of one minced, the juice of one lemon and a tablespoonful of oil if desired; decorate with tarragon tops.

129. **Spinach Salad.**—Place one pint of lettuce leaves, and one pint of tender spinach tops in a bowl with a few fresh mint leaves, dress them with oil and vinegar plain, and decorate them with sliced hard boiled eggs. A ravigote sauce is excellent with this salad.

130. **Tomato Salad.**—Slice one quart of ripe tomatoes, sprinkle with cayenne pepper, garnish with chervil or fennel, and dress with oil or lemon juice three tablespoonfuls of each.

131. **Nasturtium Salad.**—Tear two white lettuces into the salad bowl, sprinkle over them one tablespoonful of pickled nasturtiums, or capers, dress with simple oil and vinegar, and garnish with fresh nasturtium blossoms.

In mixing salad dressings, first, carefully stir together all the ingredients except the oil and vinegar, and add these gradually and alternately a few drops at a time.

132. **Cream Dressing.**—Where oil is disliked in salads the following dressing will be found excellent. Rub the yolks of two hard boiled eggs very fine with a spoon, incorporate with them a dessertspoonful of mixed

mustard, then stir in a tablespoonful of melted butter, half a teacupful of thick cream, a saltspoonful of salt, and cayenne pepper enough to take up on the point of a very small pen-knife blade, and a few drops of anchovy or Worcestershire sauce; add very carefully sufficient vinegar to reduce the mixture to a smooth creamy consistency; and pour it upon lettuce carefully prepared for the table.

133. **English Salad Sauce.**—Break the yolk of one hard boiled egg with a silver fork, add to it a saltspoonful of salt, a teaspoonful of dry mustard, a mashed mealy potato, two dessertspoonfuls each of cream and oil, and one tablespoonful of vinegar; mix until smooth and firm.

134. **Remolade.**—Beat a fresh raw egg, add to it a teaspoonful of mixed mustard, and three tablespoonfuls of oil; when smooth add just enough vinegar to change the color slightly.

135. **Sweet Sauce.**—Mix well two tablespoonfuls of oil, the raw yolk of one egg, a saltspoonful of salt, a half that quantity of pepper, one tablespoonful of vinegar, and a dessertspoonful of moist sugar.

136. **Piquante Salad Sauce.**—Mix together the yolks of two hard boiled and two raw eggs; add one tablespoonful each of cream and oil; and, when smooth, enough Chili or tarragon vinegar to season sharply, about two tablespoonfuls.

137. **Green Remolade.**—One dessertspoonful each of chopped tarragon, chives, and sorrel, pounded in a mortar; add a saltspoonful of salt, half that quantity of mignonette pepper, one tablespoonful of mixed mustard, a gill of oil, and the raw yolks of three eggs; when pounded quite smooth, dilute it with a little vinegar, and strain it through a sieve.

138. **Oil Sauce.**—Pound in a mortar one shallot or two button onions, the yolks of two hard boiled eggs, a saltspoonful of herbs, a tablespoonful of vinegar, and enough oil to thicken it, about one gill.

139. **Ravigote Sauce.**—Clean and chop a few salad herbs, put one teaspoonful of each into a small pan with a tablespoonful of meat jelly or thick stock, and a little pepper and salt; stir till the jelly is hot, and then add one tablespoonful of vinegar, and two of good oil; when thoroughly mixed

set the sauce-pan into a cool place, or pour out the mixture on a dish until it is wanted for use.

140. **Egg Dressing.**—Chop the yolks and whites of two hard boiled eggs separately, but not fine; strew them upon any salad after having dressed it with two tablespoonfuls of cream, and one of white vinegar.

141. **Anchovy Salad Sauce.**—Mix until smooth two raw eggs, one teaspoonful of the essence of anchovy, one tablespoonful of vinegar, and two of oil.

142. **Swiss Dressing.**—Pound two ounces of old cheese in a mortar, add one tablespoonful of vinegar, a little salt and pepper, and dilute to the consistency of cream with oil.

143. **Spring Dressing.**—Beat the yolks of two raw eggs, add a teaspoonful of salt, and a saltspoonful of dry mustard, chop one leek or two new onions, and mix them in, then add three tablespoonfuls of oil and one of vinegar and mix thoroughly; tear up two heads of lettuce, putting thin slices of boiled beets upon it, and pour the dressing over all.

144. **Mayonnaise.**—Place in the bottom of a salad bowl the yolk of one raw egg, a level teaspoonful of salt, the same quantity of dry mustard, a saltspoonful of white pepper, as much cayenne as can be taken up on the point of a very small pen-knife blade, and the juice of half a lemon; mix these ingredients with a wooden salad spoon until they assume a creamy white appearance; then add, drop by drop, three gills of salad oil, stirring the *mayonnaise* constantly; if it thickens too rapidly, thin it with a little of the juice from the second half of the lemon, until all is used; and towards the finish add gradually four tablespoonfuls of tarragon vinegar. Keep it cool until wanted for use.

145. **Hot Salad Sauce.**—This sauce when cold is an excellent and economical substitute for the more expensive *mayonnaise*.

Part 1.—Put one ounce each of butter and flour into a sauce-pan over the fire, and stir until it is melted, add gradually half a pint of boiling water, season with a teaspoonful of salt, and quarter of a saltspoonful of white pepper, stir till smooth, and set a little away from the fire, while you make the following sauce.

CHAPTER IX.

VEGETABLES.

Soft water is the best for boiling all vegetables. Fresh vegetables boil in one-third less time than stale ones. Green vegetables should be put into plenty of boiling water and salt, and boiled rapidly, without covering, only until tender enough to pierce with the finger nail; a bit of common washing soda, or of carbonate of ammonia, as large as a dried pea, put into the boiling water with any of the vegetables except beans, counteracts any excess of mineral elements in them, and helps to preserve their color. A lump of loaf sugar boiled with turnips neutralizes their excessive bitterness. Cabbage, potatoes, carrots, turnips, parsnips, onions, and beets, are injured by being boiled with fresh meat, and they also hurt the color of the meat, and impair its tenderness and flavor. When vegetables are cooked for use with salt meat, the meat should first be cooked and taken from the pot liquor, and the vegetables boiled in the latter. The following table will be a guide in boiling vegetables, but it must be remembered that the youngest and freshest boil in the least time; and that in winter all the roots except potatoes require nearly double the time to cook, that they would take in summer, when they are new; spinach, ten to fifteen minutes; brussels sprouts, peas, cauliflowers, and asparagus, fifteen to twenty minutes; potatoes, cabbage, corn, and string-beans, twenty to thirty minutes; turnips, onions, and squash, twenty to forty minutes; beets, carrots, and parsnips, about one hour.

147. **Asparagus with Melted Butter.**—Trim the white tough ends from two bunches of asparagus, tie it in packages of about a dozen stalks each; put them into three quarts of boiling water, with three tablespoonfuls of salt, and boil them gently until done, about twenty minutes; meantime make some drawn butter according to receipt for caper sauce, omitting the capers; fit two slices of toast to the bottom of the dish you intend to use, dip it for one instant in the water in which the asparagus has been boiled, lay it on the dish, and arrange the asparagus in a ring on it with the heads in the centre; send the butter to the table in a gravy boat, with the dish of asparagus.

148. **Green Peas.**—Boil two quarts of freshly shelled peas in two quarts of boiling water with half an ounce of butter, one bunch of green mint, and one teaspoonful each of sugar and salt, until they begin to sink to the bottom of the sauce-pan: drain them in a colander, season them with a saltspoonful of salt, and a quarter of a saltspoonful of pepper, and send them to the table hot.

149. **String Beans.**—These beans are generally marketed while they are unripe, and cooked in the shell; in that condition two quarts of them should be stringed, split in halves, cut in pieces two inches long, and thrown into boiling water with a tablespoonful of salt, *but no soda or ammonia should be added, as its action discolors them*; a few sprigs of parsley and an ounce of pork can be boiled with them to their improvement; when they are tender, which will be in about half an hour, they should be drained, and served with melted butter, made as for caper sauce, but without the capers.

150. **Baked Beets.**—Clean eight smooth beets with a soft cloth or brush; bake them in a moderate oven about one hour; rub off the skin, baste them with butter and lemon juice, return them to the oven for five minutes, and serve them hot.

151. **Brussels Sprouts.**—Trim two quarts of Brussels sprouts, wash them thoroughly, put them in three quarts of boiling water with two tablespoonfuls of salt, and boil them gently until tender, about fifteen minutes, shaking the sauce-pan occasionally; then drain them in a colander, being careful not to break them; put them again into the sauce-pan with one ounce of butter, a teaspoonful of lemon juice, a saltspoonful of salt, and quarter of a saltspoonful of white pepper; toss them gently over the fire, while you make some rounds of buttered toast for the bottom of a platter; when this is ready shake the Brussels sprouts upon it, and serve hot. Some persons like the addition of two ounces of grated Parmesan cheese; and others serve them with the *Béchamel* sauce named in receipt No. 84.

152. **Stuffed Cabbage.**—Cut the leaves of a large white cabbage as whole as possible, cut out the stalks, wash the leaves well, and boil them *only until tender*, in three quarts of boiling water and salt, with a piece of soda as large as a dried pea; have ready some sausage meat highly seasoned, and as soon as the cabbage is tender carefully drain it in a colander, run cold water

from the faucet over it, and, without tearing the leaves, lay them open on the table, two or three upon each other, making eight or ten piles. Divide the sausage meat, and lay a portion in the centre of each, fold the cabbage over it in a compact roll and tie it in place with cord; lay the rolls on a baking sheet, season with salt and pepper, put over each a tablespoonful of any rich brown gravy and brown a little in a quick oven; serve at once, on small rounds of toast.

153. **Red Cabbage.**—Cut a firm head of red cabbage in shreds, lay it in a sauce-pan with the following ingredients; one gill of vinegar, one teaspoonful each of ground cloves and salt, half a saltspoonful of pepper, two ounces of butter, and two ounces of sugar; stew it gently until tender, about one hour, shaking the pan to prevent burning, and serve it hot.

154. **Baked Cauliflower.**—Thoroughly wash a large cauliflower, boil it in plenty of boiling water and salt, until tender, about twenty minutes; drain it whole; pour over it one gill of *Béchamel* sauce, made as in receipt No. 84, dust it thickly with cracker dust, or bread crumbs, and Parmesan cheese, mixed in equal proportions, and brown it ten minutes in a quick oven.

155. **Baked Turnips.**—Pare six large yellow turnips, slice them, and boil them till tender in plenty of salted water; drain them, put them on a flat dish in layers, pour over them half a pint of *Béchamel* sauce, dust them thickly with crumbs and grated Parmesan cheese; brown them in a quick oven, and serve hot.

156. **Glazed Onions.**—Pare three dozen button onions, put them on a tin dish, pour over them a very little Spanish sauce or brown gravy, just enough to moisten them, season them with a teaspoonful of salt, and quarter of a saltspoonful of pepper; brown them in a quick oven, shaking them occasionally to color them equally; serve hot.

157. **Mushroom Pudding.**—Cleanse a quart of fresh mushrooms, cut them in small pieces, mix them with half a pound of minced ham or bacon, season them with a teaspoonful of salt, and half a saltspoonful of pepper; spread them on a roly-poly crust made by mixing one pound of flour, half a pound of shortening, and a teaspoonful of salt, with about one pint of water: roll up the crust, tie it tightly in a floured cloth, and boil it about two hours in boiling stock, or salted water; serve hot with bread, or vegetables.

158. **Boiled Potatoes.**—Potatoes should be prepared for boiling by first carefully washing them, removing the deep eyes or defective parts, and then paring off one ring all around the potato; place them in cold water with a little salt; when cooked, which will be in from twenty to thirty minutes, pour off all the water, cover them with a clean, coarse towel, *leaving off the lid of the pot*, and set them on a hot brick on the back of the fire to steam. Potatoes treated in this way can be kept fresh, hot and mealy for hours. Medium-sized and smooth potatoes are the most economical to use, and the kind should be selected in reference to the season.

159. **Lyonnaise Potatoes.**—Chop two ounces of onion, and fry it pale yellow in two ounces of butter; meantime peel boiled potatoes, either hot or cold, cut them in slices, put them into the pan containing the onion and butter, season them with a teaspoonful of salt, and half a saltspoonful of pepper, fry them pale brown, shaking the pan to prevent burning, and tossing it to brown them evenly; sprinkle with two tablespoonfuls of chopped parsley, and serve at once.

160. **Stuffed Potatoes.**—Wash twelve large potatoes with a brush; bake them *only until they begin to soften*; not more than half an hour; cut off one end, scoop out the inside with a teaspoon into a sauce-pan containing two ounces of butter, one saltspoonful of white pepper, one teaspoonful of salt, and two ounces of grated Parmesan cheese; stir all these ingredients over the fire until they are scalding hot; then fill the potato skins with the mixture, put on the ends, press the potatoes gently in shape, heat them in the oven, and serve them on a hot dish covered with a napkin, the potatoes being laid on the napkin. *Observe never to cover a baked potato unless you want it to be heavy and moist.*

161. **Potato Snow.**—Peel a quart of white potatoes, and boil them as directed in receipt No. 158; drain them thoroughly, put them in a sieve over the dish in which they are to be served, and rub them through it with a potato masher, or a wooden spoon; do not stir them after they are put into the dish, and serve them hot.

162. **Bermuda or New Potatoes.**—Wash a quart of new potatoes thoroughly, put them into plenty of boiling water and salt, and boil them until tender enough to pierce easily with a fork; drain off the water, cover

them with a towel, let them steam five minutes, and serve them in their jackets.

163. **Broiled Potatoes.**—Boil a quart of even sized potatoes until tender, but do not let them grow mealy; drain off the water, peel the potatoes, cut them in half inch slices, dip them in melted butter, and broil them over a moderate fire; serve hot, with a little butter melted.

164. **Saratoga Potatoes.**—Peel a quart of potatoes, cut them in very thin slices, and lay them in cold water and salt for an hour or more; then dry them on a towel, throw them into a deep kettle of smoking hot fat, and fry them light brown; take them out of the fat with a skimmer into a colander, scatter over them a teaspoonful of salt, shake them well about, and turn them on a platter to serve.

165. **Broiled Tomatoes.**—Wipe half a dozen large red tomatoes, cut them in half inch slices, dip them in melted butter, season them with salt and pepper, dip them in cracker crumbs, and broil them on an oiled gridiron over a moderate fire, being very careful not to break the slices in turning them. Serve them with chops for breakfast.

166. **Stuffed Tomatoes.**—Cut off the tops from eight or ten large smooth round tomatoes; scoop out the inside, and put it into a sauce-pan with quarter of a pound of scraps of ham, bacon or tongue minced fine, a saltspoonful of salt, two ounces of butter, half an ounce of chopped parsley, and four ounces of grated cheese and bread crumbs mixed; stir these ingredients over the fire until they are scalding hot, fill the tomato skins with this forcemeat, fit them neatly together, dust them with sifted bread crumbs, put over each a very little sweet oil to prevent burning, brown them in a quick oven, and serve them on a hot dish with their own gravy turned over them.

167. **Saratoga Onions.**—Slice half a dozen delicately flavored onions in small strips; drop them into plenty of smoking hot fat, fry them pale brown, and drain them for a moment in a colander. Serve hot for breakfast or lunch.

168. **Fried Beans.**—Fry two ounces of chopped onions in one ounce of butter until golden brown; put into them about a quart of cold boiled white beans, season them with a teaspoonful of salt, and half a saltspoonful of

pepper, moisten them with half a pint of any brown gravy, and serve them hot.

169. **Ham and Beans.**—Put into a sauce-pan two ounces of butter, half a saltspoonful each of salt and pepper, one quart of cold beans, and quarter of a pound of ham chopped fine; moisten these ingredients with a little gravy of any kind, heat them thoroughly, and serve at once.

170. **Kolcannon.**—Mince an ounce of onion, fry it pale yellow in one ounce of butter, add to it equal parts of cold boiled potatoes and cabbage, season with a teaspoonful of salt, and half a saltspoonful of pepper, and fry for fifteen minutes; serve hot for breakfast or lunch.

171. **Carrot Stew.**—Clean, boil, and quarter three large carrots; cut the pieces in two; simmer them gently in milk enough to cover them, season with a teaspoonful of salt, and a saltspoonful of pepper; when they are quite tender take them off the fire long enough to stir in the raw yolk of an egg, return them to the fire two minutes to cook the egg, and serve them hot at once.

172. **Baked Mushrooms.**—Clean a quart of medium sized mushrooms, trim off the roots, dip them first in some *maître d'hotel* butter made of equal parts of chopped parsley, lemon juice, and sweet butter, then roll them in cracker or bread crumbs, lay them on a dish, and just brown them in a quick oven.

173. **Stuffed Lettuce.**—Choose four round firm heads of lettuce, first bring them to a boil in hot water and salt, drain them carefully, cut out the stalk end, fill the inside of the head with minced veal or chicken highly seasoned, lay them on a baking pan, put a tablespoonful of some brown gravy over each, and then bake in a moderate oven about fifteen minutes.

174. **Stewed Parsnips.**—Wash eight parsnips, carefully cut each in four pieces, boil them in plenty of water, until tender, from twenty minutes to an hour, according to the season; then drain off the water, make a layer of quarter of a pound of salt pork on the bottom of the pot, put the parsnips in again, and fry them until brown; serve the pork with them on a platter.

CHAPTER X.

CHEAP DISHES WITHOUT MEAT.

"Bread is the staff of life;" in all ages and countries farinaceous foods have formed the bulk of man's sustenance; under this general term we include macaroni, which contains more gluten than bread and consequently is more nourishing, the different wheat flours, oat and barley meal, pearl barley, peas, beans, and lentils; the latter are the nearest article to meat in point of nourishment, containing heat-food in quantity nearly equal to wheat, and twice as much flesh food. Lentils have been used for food in older countries from time immemorial, and it is quite time that we should become acquainted with their merits; a lentil soup is given in the second chapter, and in this we append some excellent directions for cooking this invaluable food. One quart of lentils when cooked will make four pounds of hearty food. There are two varieties in market; the small flat brown seed, called lentils *à la reine*; and a larger kind, about the size of peas, and of a greenish color; both sorts are equally well flavored and nutritious. There is no reason why, with judicious seasoning, the "dinner of herbs" should lack the gustatory enjoyment which is popularly supposed to belong to the repast furnished by the "stalled ox;" especially if we are economical enough to save towards making it any pot-liquor, or cold meat gravy or drippings, which are left from a feast-day.

175. **Potato Soup.**—Slice six onions, fry them brown with two ounces of drippings, then add two ounces of flour and brown it; add four quarts of boiling water, and stir till the soup boils; season with a level tablespoonful of salt, half a saltspoonful of pepper; add one quart of potatoes peeled and cut fine, and boil all until they are tender; then stir in four ounces of oatmeal mixed smooth with a pint of cold water, and boil fifteen minutes; this soup should be stirred often enough to prevent burning; when it is nearly done mix together off the fire one ounce each of butter and flour, and stir them into the soup; when it boils up pass through a sieve with a wooden spoon, and serve hot with plenty of bread.

176. **Scotch Crowdie.**—Boil one pound of oatmeal one hour in four quarts of any kind of pot-liquor, stirring often enough to prevent burning; season with one tablespoonful of salt, a level saltspoonful of pepper, one ounce of butter, and serve with plenty of bread.

177. **Peas-pudding.**—Soak three pints of dried peas in cold water over night; tie them loosely in a clean cloth, and boil them about two hours in pot-liquor or water, putting them into it cold and bringing them gradually to a boil; drain them, pass them through a sieve with a wooden spoon, season them with a level tablespoonful of salt, half a saltspoonful of pepper, one ounce of butter, and one egg, if it is on hand; mix, tie in a clean cloth, and boil half an hour longer; then turn it from the cloth, on a dish, and serve hot.

178. **Red Herrings with Potatoes.**—Soak a dozen herrings in cold water for one hour; dry and skin them, split them down the back, and lay them in a pan with two ounces of drippings, two ounces of onion chopped fine, a saltspoonful of pepper, and three tablespoonfuls of vinegar; and set them in a moderate oven to brown for ten or fifteen minutes: meantime, boil one quart of potatoes, with a ring of the paring taken off, in plenty of boiling water and salt, pouring off the water as soon as they are tender, and letting them stand on the back of the fire, covered with a dry towel, for five minutes; serve them with the herrings, taking care to dish both quite hot.

179. **Oatmeal Porridge.**—Boil two ounces of chopped onion in two quarts of skim milk; mix half a pound of oatmeal smooth with about a pint of milk, pour it into the boiling milk, season it with a tablespoonful of salt, boil it about twenty minutes, stirring to prevent burning, and serve hot.

180. **Cheese Pudding.**—Into two quarts of boiling water, containing two tablespoonfuls of salt, stir one pound of yellow Indian meal, and three quarters of a pound of grated cheese; boil it for twenty minutes, stirring it occasionally to prevent burning; then put it in a buttered baking pan, sprinkle over the top quarter of a pound of grated cheese, and brown in a quick oven. Serve hot. If any remains, slice it cold and fry it brown.

181. **Polenta.**—Boil one pound of yellow Indian meal for half an hour, in two quarts of pot-liquor, stirring it occasionally to prevent burning; then bake it for half an hour in a buttered baking dish, and serve it either hot; or, when cold, slice it and fry it in smoking hot fat. This favorite Italian dish is

closely allied to the hasty-pudding of New England, whose praises have been sung by poe-tasters.

182. **Fish Pudding.**—Make a plain paste by mixing quarter of a pound of lard or sweet drippings with half a pound of flour, a teaspoonful of salt, and just water enough to make a stiff paste; roll it out; line the edges of a deep pudding dish with it half way down; fill the dish with layers of fresh codfish cut in small pieces, using two or three pounds, season each layer with salt, pepper, chopped parsley, and chopped onions, using one tablespoonful of salt, one saltspoonful of pepper, two bay leaves, a saltspoonful of thyme, four ounces of onion, and half an ounce of parsley; fill up the dish with any cold gravy, milk, or water, cover with paste, and bake fifteen minutes in a quick oven; finish by baking half an hour in a moderate oven; serve hot.

183. **Lentils boiled plain.**—Wash two pounds of lentils well in cold water, put them over the fire, in four quarts of cold water with one ounce of drippings, one tablespoonful of salt, and a saltspoonful of pepper, and boil slowly until tender, that is about three hours; drain off the little water which remains, add to the lentils one ounce of butter, a tablespoonful of chopped parsley, a teaspoonful of sugar, and a little more salt and pepper if required, and serve them hot. Always save the water in which they are boiled; with the addition of a little thickening and seasoning, it makes a very nourishing soup.

184. **Stewed Lentils.**—Put plain boiled lentils into a sauce-pan, cover them with any kind of pot-liquor, add one ounce of chopped onion, two ounces of butter, quarter of an ounce of chopped parsley, and stew gently for twenty minutes; serve hot.

185. **Fried Lentils.**—Fry one ounce of chopped onion brown in two ounces of drippings, add plain boiled lentils, see if they are properly seasoned, and brown them well; serve hot.

186. **Norfolk Dumplings.**—Mix well together two pounds of flour, one dessertspoonful of salt, and two pints of milk; divide the dough in twelve equal parts, and drop them into a pot of boiling pot-liquor, or boiling water; boil them steadily half an hour. They should be eaten hot, with gravy, sweet drippings, or a little molasses.

187. **Salt Cod with Parsnips.**—Soak three pounds of salt fish over night, with the skin uppermost, and boil it about one hour, putting it into plenty of cold water. Meantime pare half a dozen parsnips, and cut them in quarters, boil them half an hour, or longer, until tender, drain them, and dish them around the fish. While the fish and parsnips are cooking make the following sauce: mix two ounces of flour and one ounce of butter or sweet drippings, over the fire until a smooth paste is formed; then pour in half a pint of boiling water gradually, stirring until the sauce is smooth, add three tablespoonfuls of vinegar, season with one saltspoonful of salt, and half that quantity of pepper; let the sauce boil up thoroughly for about three minutes, and serve it with the fish and parsnips. A hard boiled egg chopped and added to the sauce improves it.

188. **Pickled Mackerel.**—When fresh mackerel or herrings can be bought cheap, clean enough to fill a two quart deep jar, pack them in it in layers with a seasoning of a tablespoonful of salt, a teaspoonful of powdered herbs a saltspoonful each of pepper and allspice, and cover with vinegar and cold water, in equal parts. Bake about one hour in a moderate oven. Serve with plain boiled potatoes.

189. **Potato Pudding.**—Wash and peel two quarts of potatoes; peel and slice about six ounces of onions; skin and bone two bloaters or large herrings; put all these ingredients in a baking dish in layers seasoning them with a dessertspoonful of salt and a saltspoonful of pepper; pour over them any cold gravy you have on hand, or add two or three ounces of drippings; if you have neither of these, water will answer; bake the pudding an hour and a half; serve hot, with bread.

CHAPTER XI.

CHEAP DISHES WITH MEAT.

Those parts of meat which are usually called inferior, and sold at low rates, such as the head, tongue, brains, pluck, tripe, feet, and tail, can be cooked so as to become both nourishing and delicate. They are more generally eaten in Europe than in this country, and they are really worthy of careful preparation; for instance, take the haslet *ragout,* the receipt for which is given further on in this chapter. The author owes this receipt to the fortunate circumstance of one day procuring a calf's liver direct from the slaughter-house, with the heart and lights attached; the liver was to be larded and cooked as directed in receipt No. 53, at a cooking lesson; the *chef* said, after laying aside the liver, "I will make for myself a dish of what the ladies would not choose," and at the direction of the author he cooked it before the class; the ladies tasted and approved. The nutritive value and flavor of the dishes specified in this chapter are less than those of prime cuts of meat, but properly combined with vegetables and cereals, they completely take the place of those more expensive foods; they should be thoroughly cooked, and well masticated; and can usually be digested with greater ease than the more solid flesh.

190. **Three dishes from a Neck of Mutton.**—PART I.—BARLEY BROTH WITH VEGETABLES.—Trim a neck of mutton into neat cutlets, and reserve them for *part 2*; put the bones and trimmings into three quarts of cold water, boil slowly, and skim thoroughly: add six ounces of barley which has been soaked in cold water over night, a bouquet of sweet herbs, two teaspoonfuls of salt, and one saltspoonful of pepper, and simmer for two hours; strain out one quart of the broth for *part 3*, then add six ounces of carrots, four ounces of onions, and four ounces of yellow turnips cut in dice about half an inch square, six ounces of oatmeal mixed to a smooth batter with cold water, and simmer until the vegetables are tender, which will be about half an hour: taste to try the seasoning and serve hot.—PART II.—MUTTON STEW.—Cut half a quart each of yellow turnips and potatoes into balls as large as marbles, saving the trimmings to put into soup, and for mashed potatoes;

peel six ounces of small onions; put all these in separate vessels to boil until tender enough to pierce with a fork; meantime put the cutlets in a hot pan containing an ounce of drippings, and fry them brown quickly; stir among them one ounce of dry flour; brown it, add one quart of boiling water; season with one teaspoonful of salt, and a quarter of a saltspoonful of pepper; drain the vegetables, put them with the meat and gravy, and serve hot.—PART III.—FRIED PUDDING.—To the quart of broth strained off as directed in *Part I*, and brought to the boiling point, gradually add sufficient Indian meal to thicken it, about half a pound will generally be enough; season with a teaspoonful of salt, and boil it for twenty minutes, stirring it occasionally to prevent burning; pour it out into a deep earthen dish, and let it stand long enough to grow solid; then cut it in slices, and fry it brown in drippings; it can be eaten with molasses for dessert. With proper management all these dishes can be ready at one time, and will form a good and wholesome dinner.

191. **Neck of Pork stuffed.**—Clean a neck of fresh pork, fill it with sage and onion stuffing, made according to receipt No. ——; put it in a dripping pan, with some small potatoes, peeled and washed well in cold water, roast it brown, seasoning with a teaspoonful of salt, and half a saltspoonful of pepper, when it is half done; when it is thoroughly cooked serve it with the potatoes laid around it, and a gravy made from the drippings in the pan cleared of fat, and thickened with a teaspoonful of flour.

192. **Pigs' Feet Fried.**—Thoroughly burn all the hairs off with a poker heated to a white heat; then scald the feet, wipe them dry, and put them over the fire to boil in cold water, with two ounces each of carrot and onion, the latter stuck with six cloves, two tablespoonfuls of salt, quarter of an ounce of parsley made into a bouquet with three bay leaves and a sprig of thyme; boil them slowly four hours, or more, until you can easily remove the bones. Split the feet in two pieces, and take out all the large bones; have ready some sifted crumbs of cracker, or dry bread, a little milk, or an egg beaten with a teaspoonful of water; dry the pieces on a clean towel, roll them first in the crumbs, then dip them in the milk or egg, and roll them again in the crumbs; fry them in smoking hot lard, which you must afterwards strain and save to use again, and lay them neatly on a hot dish; they will make an appetizing and nourishing meal.

193. **Pigs' Tongue and Brains.**—Soak them in cold water with two tablespoonfuls of salt for two hours; then put them into cold water over the fire, with two ounces each of carrot and onion, the latter stuck with three cloves, a bouquet of sweet herbs, and a tablespoonful of vinegar, and boil slowly fifteen minutes; take out the brains leaving the tongue still boiling, and put them in cold water to cool; then carefully remove the thin membrane or skin covering the brains, without breaking them; season them with a saltspoonful of salt and quarter of a saltspoonful of pepper, roll them in cracker crumbs, and fry them brown in smoking hot fat. By this time the tongue will be tender; take it up, lay it on a dish between the brains, put a few sprigs of parsley, celery, mint or watercresses, around them and serve them hot. This inexpensive dish is very delicate and nutritious.

194. **Roasted Tripe.**—Cut some tripe in pieces three inches long by six wide; cover each one with highly seasoned sausage-meat, roll up, and tie with a string; lay the rolls in a dripping pan, dredge them well with flour, and set them in the oven to bake, basting them with the liquor which flows from them; when they are nicely browned, dish them up with a slice of lemon on each one. Some melted butter may be put over them if desired.

195. **Ragout of Haslet.**—Wash the lights, cut them in two inch pieces, put them into a sauce-pan with one ounce each of butter, salt pork sliced, onion chopped, one dessertspoonful of salt, and half a saltspoonful of black pepper; two bay leaves, two sprigs of parsley and one of thyme, tied in a bouquet, one ounce of flour, one gill of vinegar, half a pint of cold gravy or cold water, and six potatoes peeled and cut in dice; stew all these ingredients gently together for two hours, and serve as you would a stew, with a tablespoonful of chopped parsley sprinkled over the top.

196. **Cock-a-leeky.**—Pluck, singe, and draw a cheap fowl, as directed in receipt No. ——; break the breast bone down with a rolling-pin, tie the fowl in a plump shape, put it into a sauce-pan with four quarts of cold water, one pound of rice, first washed in cold water, a tablespoonful of salt, half a saltspoonful of pepper, and a bunch of leeks weighing about a pound, cut in two-inch pieces. Boil all gently for three hours, stirring occasionally to prevent the rice burning; serve the fowl on one dish with a tablespoonful of parsley chopped and sprinkled over it, and the rice and broth in a soup tureen or deep dish.

197. **Italian Cheese.**—Chop a pig's pluck, and two pounds of scraps or trimmings of fresh pork, season this forcemeat to taste with the spice salt of mixed spices and sweet herbs named in Chapter first; put it into an earthen jar with a lid, seal the lid with a paste made of flour and water, and oiled upon the surface to prevent cracking; put the jar in a moderate oven, and bake the cheese three hours, slowly. This dish is eaten cold with bread, in place of butter, and makes a hearty meal.

198. **Gammon Dumpling.**—Make a plain paste of two pounds of flour, one dessertspoonful of salt, half a pound of finely chopped suet or scraps, and sufficient cold water to mix it to a stiff dough; roll this out about half an inch thick, spread over it about two pounds of any cheap cut of bacon or ham, finely chopped, roll up the dumpling as you would a roly-poly pudding, tie it tightly in a clean cloth, and boil it in boiling water, or boiling pot-liquor, for about three hours. Serve it hot, with plain boiled potatoes.

199. **Toad-in-the-Hole.**—Cut two pounds of the cheapest parts of any good meat into small pieces, roll them in flour, pepper, and salt, and fry them brown in two ounces of drippings; meantime prepare a batter as follows; mix one pound of flour, one heaping teaspoonful of salt, half a nutmeg grated, and two eggs, stirred in without beating; gradually add three pints of skim-milk, making a smooth batter; add the meat and its gravy to this batter, put it in a greased baking dish, and bake it slowly about two hours. Serve it with plain boiled potatoes.

200. **Bacon Roly-Poly.**—Boil a pound and a half of bacon for half an hour; then slice it thin; peel and slice six apples and the same number of onions; make a stiff dough of two pounds of flour, a teaspoonful of salt, and cold water; roll it out half an inch thick; lay the bacon, apples, and onion all over it, roll it up, tie it tightly in a clean cloth, and boil it about two hours, in plenty of boiling water. Serve it with boiled potatoes, or boiled cabbage.

201. **Baked Ox-heart.**—Clean the heart thoroughly; stuff it with the following forcemeat; one ounce of onion chopped fine, a tablespoonful of chopped parsley, a saltspoonful of powdered sage or thyme, a teaspoonful of salt, half a small loaf of bread, and enough warm water to moisten the bread; mix, stuff the heart with it, and bake it an hour in a good hot oven, basting it occasionally with the liquor that flows from it, and when half

done seasoning it well with salt and pepper. Serve hot with plain boiled potatoes, or with potatoes peeled, and baked in the pan with the heart.

202. **Tripe and Onions.**—Cut two pounds of tripe in pieces two inches square; peel and slice six large onions and ten potatoes; slice a quarter of a pound of salt pork or bacon; put the bacon in the bottom of a pot, with the tripe and vegetables in layers on it, seasoning with a tablespoonful of salt, a saltspoonful of pepper, and the same of powdered herbs; mix a pound of flour gradually with a quart and a half of cold water, pour it over the tripe and vegetables, and boil it gently for two hours. Serve hot with bread.

203. **Peas and Bacon.**—Cut a quarter of a pound of fat bacon in small bits, and fry it brown with two ounces of onions sliced; then add four ounces of split peas, one tablespoonful of salt, one saltspoonful of pepper, one teaspoonful of sugar, and four quarts of cold water; boil it until the peas are reduced to a pulp, which will be about three hours; then stir in sufficient oatmeal to thicken it, and boil slowly twenty minutes, stirring it occasionally; serve hot; or when cold, slice and fry it brown.

204. **Pot-au-feu.**—Put into four quarts of cold water one pound of cheap lean meat, and one pound of liver whole, some bones, cut into bits, two tablespoonfuls of salt, one teaspoonful of pepper, four leeks cut in pieces, and the following vegetables whole; four carrots, four turnips, and four onions, each stuck with two cloves; boil all gently for three hours, skimming occasionally, and adding two tablespoonfuls of cold water about every half hour; take up the meat and the liver on a platter, arrange the vegetables neatly around them, and serve the broth in a tureen, with plenty of bread.

205. **Ragout of Mutton.**—Cut four pounds of the scrag end of mutton in small pieces; peel a quart of turnips and cut them in round pieces as large as a walnut, and fry them brown in four ounces of fat; take them up, mix into the fat four ounces of flour, and brown it; add the mutton and sufficient cold water to cover the meat, and stir until it boils; season with a tablespoonful of salt, half a saltspoonful of pepper, a teaspoonful of sugar, and an ounce of onion if the flavor is liked; simmer gently until the meat is tender, about two hours; then add the turnips, heat them, and serve hot.

CHAPTER XII.

THE CHILDREN'S CHAPTER.

Any elaborate discussion of the relations of food to the needs of the body would not come within the scope of a work of this character; but there are a few facts concerning the diet of children to which we would call the attention of those mothers who wish their little brood to brighten home with radiant eyes, rosy cheeks, plump, graceful forms, and hearts bubbling over with the vivacity which springs from perfect health. Let them discard sago, arrowroot, and tapioca, all largely composed of starch, as comparatively useless in nourishing the growing body, which calls for the most complete nutrients; these often do very well in illness, where no great degree of nourishment is necessary, and where simply a given quantity of bland, innutritious food is required to help the system do without stronger aliment, calculated to irritate overworked and sensitive organs.

Indigestible articles, such as fat meat, rich pastry, hot bread, unripe fruit and vegetables, tea, coffee, spices, and stimulants, should be avoided in the diet of children. Good wheaten bread, farina, ripe fruit, fresh vegetables, meat-juices, milk, and sugar, should make up the list of staples; when meats are used they should be nutritious and digestible, such as good mutton, young beef, and tender poultry; bread and milk and fruit, for breakfast; meat, vegetables, bread and some light dessert, for dinner; bread and milk, or their equivalents, for supper; in other words, plain food and plenty of it, will keep mind and body in a sound condition, and supply all the requirements of growth.

Meats should be carefully cooked, so as to preserve all their natural juices; but no rich sauces, or made gravies, should accompany them to the table; a few ripe vegetables cooked until perfectly tender, roasted or baked potatoes, seed-bearing fruits, generally stewed, and plenty of light bread at least a day old, should be eaten with the meat. In stewing fruit only enough water should be used to prevent burning, and plenty of sugar should be employed to sweeten it; all fruit is less apt to be injurious if eaten early in the day.

Eggs should be plain boiled, and rather soft. Milk should be boiled when there is any undue action of the bowels; otherwise it should be used uncooked with plenty of bread.

Hearty, vigorous children, who play much in the open air, can digest more meat than those who are confined indoors; and the cravings of a healthy appetite should always be appeased, care being taken that the stomach has the proper intervals of rest. Regularity of meals is really most important at all ages; the digestive organs must have time to assimilate their food supply. In childhood and youth, the period of growth, the needs of the system are more pressing than at any other time of life; if at this time children are fed on rich and stimulating food, they will be prone to fevers; if they are underfed they suffer both mentally and physically from slow starvation; equal and regular nutrition is imperative to the well being of the little ones, if we would have them grow up capable of performing in the fullest degree the highest functions of life. Therefore give the children plenty of plain, wholesome food; their active systems will appropriate it. If they continue serene in temper, equable in disposition, and generally healthy,—if the eyes are bright, the skin clear, the sleep serene,—the diet is proper and sufficient.

In the following receipts for preparing children's food the quantities are calculated for four.

206. **Oatmeal Porridge.**—Oatmeal is an extremely strengthening food; when it is well cooked it produces a large volume of nutritive matter in proportion to its bulk; and combined with milk it is the strongest and best of the cereals. Its flavor is sweet and pleasant; it appears in market in two forms, a rather rough meal, and the unbroken grain, after the husk has been removed; in either shape it should be thoroughly boiled, and combined with milk. A good thick porridge can be made by stirring four ounces of oatmeal into a quart of boiling milk, and then pouring this into a quart of water boiling on the fire, and allowing it to boil half or three-quarters of an hour; care must be taken not to burn it; just before it is done it should be seasoned with a teaspoonful of salt; and sweetened to taste at the table.

207. **A good Breakfast** can be made of fresh milk sweetened with a little sugar and eaten with bread a day old, lightly buttered.

208. **Stewed Fruit.**—Put a quart of apples pared and sliced over the fire in a thick sauce-pan, with half a pint of water, to prevent burning, and when tender break them well up and sweeten them with four ounces or more of sugar, according to the flavor of the apples. Serve them with bread and butter in the morning, or at noon.

209. **Ripe Currants.**—A pound of ripe currants mashed, and mixed with half a pound, or more, of sugar, makes an excellent accompaniment for bread, being served spread upon the slices.

210. **Blackberry Jam.**—This is an invaluable addition to the breakfast, or noon dinner, in place of butter. It is an excellent agent for regulating the action of the bowels. It is made by boiling with every pound of thoroughly ripe blackberries half a pound of good brown sugar; the boiling to be continued one hour, and the berries well broken up.

211. **Baked Fruit.**—In addition to baking apples in the ordinary way, plums, peaches, pears, and berries, are good when put into a stone jar with layers of stale bread and sugar, and about a gill of water, and baking the fruit slowly in a moderate oven for an hour and a half.

212. **Broiled Chops.**—Trim nearly all the fat from a pound of loin mutton chops, broil them over a clear, bright fire for about fifteen minutes, taking care not to burn them; when they are done put them on a hot platter, season them with half a teaspoonful of salt, and if they are very dry put a little butter over them, using not more than a quarter of an ounce. Serve them with mashed potatoes.

213. **Beefsteak.**—A tender sirloin steak is the best cut for general use. It should be chosen in accordance with the directions given in the chapter on marketing, and broiled over a brisk, clear fire for about twenty minutes; the seasoning of salt should be added after it is taken from the fire, and placed on a hot dish; and but very little butter, if any, should be used. Serve it with baked potatoes, finely broken with a fork.

214. **Broiled Chicken.**—A tender, but not very fat chicken, makes an excellent dinner for children. It should be plucked, singed, split down the back, carefully drawn, and wiped with a damp cloth, but not washed; the joints and breast-bone should be broken with the rolling pin, the chicken

being covered with a folded towel to protect the flesh; it should then be broiled, inside first, over a clear, brisk fire, or better still, laid in a pan on a couple of slices of bread, and quickly roasted in a hot oven; by the latter process all the juices of the bird are saved; some gravy will flow from a good chicken, and from this the superfluous fat should be removed; if the chicken is very fat the bread under it should not be given to the children.

215. **Boiled Eggs.**—Eggs are usually spoiled in cooking; if they are plunged into boiling water, and maintained at the boiling point, the effect is to harden the albumen while the yolk remains almost raw, and make them totally unfit for digestion. A good way to cook them is to place them over the fire in cold water, bring them slowly to a boil, and then at once set the vessel containing them back from the fire, and let the eggs stand in the water about one minute if they are to be soft, and two minutes, or longer, if they are to be hard. Poor eggs cooked in this way are superior in flavor and digestibility to new-laid eggs boiled rapidly. One minute is quite long enough to boil them if they are wanted in their best condition.

216. **Baked Potatoes.**—Potatoes for baking should be of equal and medium size, with smooth skins; they should be well washed with a brush or cloth, and put into a quick oven; they will bake in from twenty to thirty-five minutes, according to variety and ripeness; as soon as you find they yield readily when pressed between the fingers, they are done; and should be served at once, *uncovered*. If they stand they grow heavy, and if you put them in a covered dish you will make them watery.

217. **Boiled Potatoes.**—Potatoes for children's use should be very carefully boiled; and if not used as soon as they are done, should be kept hot and dry, by pouring off the water, covering them with a dry cloth, and setting them on the back of the stove. After washing them thoroughly, pare them entirely, or take off one ring around each; if they are new, put them over the fire in hot water; if they are old, put them on in cold water; in either case, add a tablespoonful of salt, and boil them from fifteen to thirty minutes, as they require, until you can pierce them easily with a fork; then drain off all the water, cover them with a clean dry towel, and set them on the back of the fire until you are ready to use them.

218. **Apple Cake.**—Grate a small loaf of stale bread; pare and slice about a quart of apples; lightly butter a pudding mould, dust it well with flour, and then with sugar, and fill it with layers of bread crumbs, apples, and sugar, using a very little cinnamon to flavor it; let the top layer be of crumbs, and put a few bits of butter on it; bake the cake for one hour in a moderate oven; and serve it for dessert.

219. **Fruit Farina.**—Sprinkle three tablespoonfuls of farina into one quart of boiling milk, using a sauce-pan set into a kettle of boiling water, in order to prevent burning; flavor and sweeten to taste, and boil for half an hour, stirring occasionally; then add one pint of any ripe berries, or sliced apples, and boil until the fruit is cooked, about twenty minutes: the pudding may be boiled in a mould or a cloth after the fruit is added. It should be served with powdered sugar.

220. **Plain Cookies.**—Beat one egg with one cup of sugar to a cream, work two ounces of butter soft, and beat it with the egg and sugar, grate in quarter of a nutmeg, add one gill of milk, and prepared flour enough to make a sufficiently stiff paste to roll out about a pound. Roll an eighth of an inch thick, cut out with a biscuit cutter, or an inverted cup, and lay on a floured baking pan, and bake about twenty minutes in a moderate oven.

221. **Plain Gingerbread.**—Partly melt one ounce of butter, stir it into half a pint of molasses, with a tablespoonful of ground ginger, and half a pint of boiling water, stir in smoothly half a pound of prepared flour, and pour the batter into a buttered baking pan; bake it about half an hour in a quick oven, trying it with a broom straw, at the end of twenty minutes; as soon as the straw passes through it without sticking, the cake is done.

222. **Strawberry Shortcake.**—Rub two ounces of butter into a pound of prepared flour, mix it stiff enough to mould with about half a pint of milk; put the dough upon a round tin plate, gently flattening with the roller; bake it about twenty minutes in a quick oven, trying it with a broom straw to be sure it is done, before taking it from the oven; let it cool a little, tear it open by first separating the edges all around with a fork, and then pulling it in two pieces; upon the bottom put a thick layer of strawberries, or any perfectly ripe fruit, plentifully sprinkled with sugar; then lay on the fruit the upper half of the shortcake, with the crust down; add another layer of fruit,

with plenty of sugar, and serve it with sweet milk or cream. This is rather rich, but a small piece may be given to the children as a treat, at the noon dinner.

223. **Apple Custard.**—Pare and core six apples; set them in a pan with a very little water, and stew them until tender; then put them in a pudding dish without breaking, fill the centres with sugar, and pour over them a custard made of a quart of milk, five eggs, four ounces of sugar, and a very little nutmeg; set the pudding-dish in a baking-pan half full of water, and bake it about half an hour. Serve it either hot or cold, at the noon dinner.

CHAPTER XIII.

COOKERY FOR INVALIDS.

224. **Diet for Invalids.**—There are three alimentary conditions in illness; the first prevails where the system suffers from the reaction consequent upon over-taxation, when rest is the first demand; then only palliative foods meet the calls of nature, those which give repletion to the sense of hunger, and tide the system over a certain period of relaxation and recuperation; gelatinous soups, and gruels of arrowroot, sago, and tapioca, will do very well at this stage. The second condition, when the body, failing under the pressure of disease, needs an excess of nutrition, is serious enough to demand the interposition of the physician—the doctor is the proper person to decide what shall be eaten; we will offer only a few suggestions concerning refreshing drinks. At the third point, when the patient is beyond the reach of danger, when foods are ordered which shall yield the greatest possible amount of nutrition, the culinary skill of the nurse may be displayed. It is here that we would give the paragraphs concerning highly nutritive foods. The reader will please to note that the quantities in this chapter are calculated for the use of one person.

225. **Gruels.**—We have already said that in certain physical conditions the lack of nutrition is what the body requires,—a period of comparative inaction, combined with repletion;—in such a condition the following aliments will suffice.

226. **Arrowroot Gruel.**—Mix one ounce of arrowroot with sufficient cold water to make a smooth paste; into this pour a gill or more of boiling water, stirring the mixture until it is quite clear; sweeten it with a little sugar, and use it at once.

227. **Arrowroot Jelly.**—Dissolve two teaspoonfuls of Bermuda arrowroot in just enough cold water to mix it to a smooth liquid paste, stir it into a quarter of a pint of water boiling upon the fire, with two tablespoonfuls of white sugar; continue stirring until the mixture becomes clear, then remove

from the fire and stir in one teaspoonful of lemon-juice, put into a mould wet with cold water until it is cold. If the patient's condition will permit, cream and sugar may be eaten with it.

228. **Arrowroot Wine Jelly.**—Following the above process, make a jelly of one cup of boiling water, two teaspoonfuls of arrowroot, two teaspoonfuls of white sugar, one tablespoonful of brandy or three tablespoonfuls of wine. This jelly is more stimulating than the gruel, and may meet some especial cases; but, unless used with brandy, for impaired digestive powers, we do not believe it to be of permanent value.

229. **Calf's Foot Jelly.**—Thoroughly clean a calf's foot; put it into an earthen jar, with half the rind of a fresh lemon, two gills of sweet milk, and one pint of cold water; close the jar tightly, put it into a moderate oven, and slowly bake it for three hours; then strain and cool it, and remove all fat, before using; it is bland and harmless.

230. **Sago Gruel.**—Soak one ounce of sago, after washing it well in a pint of tepid water for two hours; then simmer it in the same water for fifteen minutes, stirring it occasionally; then sweeten and flavor it to taste, and use at once.

231. **Sago Milk.**—Prepare the sago as in previous receipt, but boil it in milk instead of water; and when it has cooked for two hours it is ready for use.

232. **Tapioca Jelly.**—Wash one ounce of tapioca, soak it over night in cold water, and then simmer it with a bit of lemon peel until it is thoroughly dissolved; sweeten it to taste, and let it cool before using.

233. **Rice Candle.**—Mix an ounce of ground rice smoothly with a little cold water, and stir it into a pint of boiling water; boil it for fifteen minutes, and then sweeten it to taste and flavor it with nutmeg. Use it warm or cold.

234. **Isinglass Milk.**—Soak quarter of an ounce of clear shreds of isinglass in a pint of cold milk for two hours; then reduce it by boiling to half a pint, and sweeten to taste. Cool it before using.

235. **Refreshing Drinks.**—In feverish conditions cooling drinks, that is beverages which are in themselves refrigerant, such as lemonade, and those which are made from aromatic herbs, are grateful and helpful to the patient,

but pure, distilled or filtered water, is the best for invalids. Hot drinks lower the temperature of the body by evaporation; excessively cold drinks check perspiration, and endanger congestion of some vital part; but water of a moderate temperature is innocuous. Even in dangerous fevers the burning thirst of the sufferer can safely be assuaged by the frequent administration of small bits of ice. In cases of incomplete nutrition, cocoa, chocolate, and other preparations of the fruit of the cocoa-palm, are invaluable adjuncts; the active principle of all these is identical, and the chief nutritive element is oil. A very small quantity of cocoa will sustain life a long time.

236. **Filtered Water.**—Put a quart of clear water over the fire, and just bring it to a boil; remove it, and strain it three or four times through flannel; then cool it in a covered jar or pitcher, and give it to the patient in small quantities as the condition requires.

237. **Jelly Water.**—Mix one large teaspoonful of wild-cherry or blackberry jelly in a glass of cool water; drink moderately, and at intervals.

238. **Flaxseed Lemonade.**—Pour one quart of boiling water over four tablespoonfuls of whole flaxseed, and steep three hours covered. Then sweeten to taste, and add the juice of two lemons, using a little more water if the liquid seems too thick to be palatable. This beverage is very soothing to the irritated membranes in cases of severe cold.

239. **Barley Water.**—Wash two ounces of pearl barley in cold water until it does not cloud the water; boil it for five minutes in half a pint of water; drain that off, put the barley into two quarts of clean water, and boil it down to one quart. Cool, strain, and use. Pearl barley largely contains starch and mucilage, and makes an excellent soothing and refreshing draught in fevers and gastric inflammations.

NOURISHING DRINKS.—These are useful when liquid nourishment is better suited to the invalid's condition than solid food.

240. **Iceland Moss Chocolate.**—Dissolve one ounce of Iceland moss in one pint of boiling milk; boil one ounce of chocolate for five minutes in one pint of boiling water; thoroughly mix the two; and give it to the invalid night and morning. This is a highly nutritive drink for convalescents.

241. **Egg Broth.**—Beat an egg until it is frothy, stir into it a pint of boiling hot meat broth, free from fat, season it with a saltspoonful of salt, and eat it hot, with thin slices of dry toast; it may be given to assist the patient in gaining strength.

242. **Egg Tea.**—Beat the yolk of an egg in a cup of tea, and let the sick person drink it warm; the yolk is more readily digested than the white, and has a better flavor; and the tea is a powerful respiratory excitant, while it promotes perspiration, and aids the assimilation of more nourishing foods.

243. **Very strong Beef Tea.**—(*This tea contains every nutritious element of the beef.*)—Cut two pounds of lean beef into small dice, put it into a covered jar *without water*, and place it in a moderate oven for four hours, then strain off the gravy, and dilute it to the desired strength with boiling water.

244. **Beef Tea.**—(*A quick preparation for immediate use.*)—Chop one pound of lean beef fine, put it into a bowl, and cover it with cold water; let it stand for fifteen or twenty minutes, and then pour both beef and liquid into a sauce-pan, and place them over the fire to boil from fifteen to thirty minutes as time will permit; then strain off the liquid, season it slightly, and serve it at once.

245. **Farina Gruel.**—Stir one ounce of farina into one pint of boiling water, and boil it down one half, using a farina kettle, or stirring occasionally to prevent burning, then add half a pint of milk, boil up once, and sweeten to taste. Use warm. Farina is a preparation of the inner portion of the finest wheat, freed from bran, and floury dust; it contains an excess of nitrogenous, or flesh-forming material, readily absorbs milk or water in the process of cooking, is quickly affected by the action of the gastric juices; and is far superior as a food to sago, arrowroot, tapioca, and corn starch.

246. **Nutritious Foods.**—We have called attention to the fact that the nurse's most important office is exercised when the invalid begins to regain health; the task of rebuilding exhausted vitality demands a thoughtful care that only a tender hearted woman can bestow; and lacking which the skill of the most enlightened physician is often set at naught. Happy the woman who can here assist the restoration of the vital powers; she holds in her own hands a force which wealth cannot buy. To such ministering angels we

dedicate this portion of our little work, in the hope that countless sick beds will be comforted thereby.

247. **Bread Jelly.**—Remove the crust from a roll, slice the crumb, and toast it; put the slices in one quart of water, and set it over the fire to simmer until it jellies; then strain it through a cloth, sweeten it, and flavor it with lemon juice; put it into a mould and cool it upon the ice before using.

248. **Crackers and Marmalade.**—Toast three soda crackers, dip them for one minute in boiling water, spread them with a little sweet butter, and put between them layers of orange marmalade, or any other preserve or jelly; put plenty upon the top cracker, and set them in the oven for two or three minutes before serving. This makes a delicate and inviting lunch for convalescents.

249. **Chicken Jelly.**—Skin a chicken, removing all fat, and break up the meat and bones by pounding; cover them with cold water, heat them slowly in a steam-tight kettle, and simmer them to a pulp; then strain through a sieve or cloth, season to taste, and return to the fire without the cover, to simmer until the liquid is reduced one half, skimming off all fat. Cool to form a jelly. If you have no steam-tight kettle, put a cloth between the lid and any kettle, and the purpose will be served.

250. **Chicken Broth.**—Dress a chicken or fowl, cut it in joints, put them in a chopping bowl, and chop them into small pieces, using flesh, bones, and skin. To every pound of the chicken thus prepared put one pint of cold water and one level teaspoonful of salt; if pepper is desired it should be either enough cayenne to lie on the point of a small pen-knife blade, or a half saltspoonful of ground *white* pepper. Put all these ingredients over the fire in a porcelain lined sauce-pan, bring them slowly to a boil, remove the pan to the side of the fire, where it will simmer slowly, the heat striking it on one side; simmer it in this way for two hours, and then strain it through a napkin, set it to cool; if any fat rises to the surface in cooling remove it entirely. Eat it either cold, say half a teacupful when a little nourishment is required; or warm a pint, and eat it with graham crackers at meal time.

251. **Beefsteak Juice.**—Quickly broil a juicy steak, and after laying it on a hot platter, cut and press it to extract all the juice; season this with a very

little salt, and pour it over a slice of delicately browned toast; serve it at once.

252. **Salmon Steak.**—Choose a slice of salmon nearly an inch thick, remove the scales, wipe with a dry cloth, roll it first in cracker dust, then dip it very lightly in melted butter, and season with a dust of white pepper and a pinch of salt; then roll it again in cracker dust, and put it over a clear fire on a greased gridiron, to broil slowly, taking care that it does not burn before the flakes separate; serve it with some fresh watercresses and plain boiled potatoes. (Any *red-blooded* fish may be used in the same way.)

253. **Broiled Oysters.**—Dry some large oysters on a napkin; roll them in cracker dust, dip them in melted butter as for salmon steaks, again in cracker dust, dust over them a very little salt and white pepper, or cayenne, and broil them on a buttered wire gridiron, over a clear fire. They will be done as soon as they are light brown. They make a very delicate and digestible meal.

CHAPTER XIV.

BREAD.

The preparation of wheat and other grains, in the form of bread, is one of the most important of all culinary operations, and to many persons one of the most difficult. It is impossible to set exact rules as to the quantity of flour or liquid to be used, for the quality of the flour varies as much as that of the grain from which it is made; and some varieties, excessive in gluten, will absorb nearly one-third more liquid than others, and produce correspondingly more bread. For this reason in buying flour we must choose that which contains the most gluten; this kind will remain in a firm, compact mass when pressed in the hand, and will retain all the lines and marks of the skin; or if mixed with water it will take up a great deal in proportion to its bulk, and will form a tough, elastic dough. Gluten in flour corresponds with the nitrates or flesh-formers in flesh, and abounds in hard winter wheat. The flour containing much of it is never extremely white.

The object of making bread, that is of mixing water with the flour and subsequently exposing the dough to intense heat, is to expand and rupture the cells of the grain so as to expose the greatest possible surface to the action of the digestive fluids; this is accomplished in several ways; by the formation of air cells through the medium of acetous fermentation, as in yeast bread; by the mechanical introduction of carbonic acid gas, as in ærated bread; by the mixture with the flour of a gas-generating compound, which needs only the contact of moisture to put it in active operation; and by the beating into the dough of atmospheric air. No organic change in the elements of the flour is necessary, like that produced by the partial decomposition of some of its properties, in bread raised with yeast; so long as proper surface is obtained for the action of the gastric juices, the purpose of raising is accomplished. Bread raised without fermentation can be made from the following receipt, and there is no question of its healthfulness.

254. **Aerated Homemade Bread.**—Mix flour and water together to the consistency of a thick batter; then beat it until fine bubbles of air thoroughly permeate it; for small biscuit, pour it into patty pans, and bake in a good

brisk oven; for bread in loaves more flour is thoroughly kneaded in with the hands, until the dough is full of air-bubbles, and then baked at once, without being allowed to stand.

When bread is to be raised by the acetous fermentation of yeast, the sponge should be maintained at a temperature of 89° Fahr. until it is sufficiently light, and the baking should be accomplished at a heat of over 320°. When yeast is too bitter from the excess of hops, mix plenty of water with it, and let it stand for some hours; then throw the water off, and use the settlings. When yeast has soured it may be restored by adding to it a little carbonate of soda or ammonia. When dough has soured, the acidity can be corrected by the use of a little carbonate of soda or ammonia. If the sponge of "raised bread" be allowed to overwork itself it will sour from excessive fermentation, and if the temperature be permitted to fall, and the dough to cool, it will be heavy. Thorough kneading renders yeast-bread white and fine, but is unnecessary in bread made with baking-powder. Great care should be taken in the preparation of yeast for leavened bread, as the chemical decomposition inseparable from its use is largely increased by any impurity or undue fermentation. Experience and judgment are necessary to the uniform production of good bread; and those are gained only by repeated trials. We subjoin one of the best receipts which we have been able to procure, for making yeast.

255. **Homebrewed Yeast.**—Boil two ounces of the best hops in four quarts of water for half an hour, strain off the liquor and let it cool till luke-warm, and then add half a pound of brown sugar and two heaping tablespoonfuls of salt; use a little of this liquor to beat up one pound of the best flour, and gradually mix in all of it with the flour; let it stand four days to ferment in a warm place near the fire, stirring it frequently. On the third day boil and mash three pounds of potatoes, and stir them into it. On the fourth day strain and bottle it; it will keep good for months.

256. **Homemade Bread.**—Put seven pounds of flour into a deep pan, and make a hollow in the centre; into this put one quart of luke-warm water, one tablespoonful of salt, one teaspoonful of sugar, and half a gill of yeast; have ready three pints more of warm water, and use as much of it as is necessary to make a rather soft dough, mixing and kneading it well with both hands. When it is smooth and shining strew a little flour upon it, lay a large towel

over it folded, and set it in a warm place by the fire for four or five hours to rise; then knead it again for fifteen minutes, cover it with the towel, and set it to rise once more; then divide it into two or four loaves, and bake it in a quick oven. This quantity of material will make eight pounds of bread, and will require one hour's baking to two pounds of dough. In cold weather, the dough should be mixed in a warm room, and not allowed to cool while rising; if it does not rise well, set the pan containing it over a large vessel of boiling water; it is best to mix the bread at night, and let it rise till morning, in a warm and even temperature.

257. **Milk Bread.**—Take one quart of milk, heat one-third of it, and scald with it half a pint of flour; if the milk is skimmed, use a small piece of butter; when the batter is cool, add the rest of the milk, one cup of hop yeast, half a tablespoonful of salt, and flour enough to make it quite stiff; knead the dough until it is fine and smooth, and raise it over night. This quantity makes three small loaves.

258. **Rice Bread.**—Simmer one pound of rice in three quarts of water until the rice is soft, and the water evaporated or absorbed; let it cool until it is only luke-warm; mix into it nearly four pounds of flour, two teaspoonfuls of salt, and four tablespoonfuls of yeast; knead it until it is smooth and shining, let it rise once before the fire, make it up into loaves with the little flour reserved from the four pounds, and bake it thoroughly.

259. **Potato Bread.**—Take good, mealy boiled potatoes, in the proportion of one-third of the quantity of flour you propose to use, pass them through a coarse sieve into the flour, using a wooden spoon and adding enough cold water to enable you to pass them through readily; use the proper quantity of yeast, salt, and water, and make up the bread in the usual way. A saving of at least twenty per cent is thus gained.

260. **Pulled Bread.**—Take from the oven an ordinary loaf of bread when it is about *half baked*, and with the fingers, *while it is yet hot*, pull it apart in egg-sized pieces of irregular shape: throw them upon tins, and bake them in a slow oven to a rich brown color. This bread is excellent to eat with cheese or wine.

Where bread is made with baking powder the following rules should be closely observed: If any shortening be used, it should be rubbed into the flour before it is wet; *cold* water or sweet milk should always be used to wet it, and the dough should be kneaded immediately, and only long enough to thoroughly mix it and form it into the desired shape; it should then be placed in a well-heated oven and baked quickly—otherwise the carbonic acid gas will escape before the expanded cells are fixed in the bread, and thus the lightness of the loaf will be impaired.

As a very large margin of profit is indulged in by the manufacturers of baking powders, we subjoin a good formula for making the article at home at a considerable saving.

261. **Baking Powder.**—Mix thoroughly by powdering and sifting together several times the following ingredients; four ounces of tartaric acid, and six ounces each of bi-carbonate of soda, and starch. Keep the mixture in an air-tight can.

The following receipts will be found useful and easy:

262. **Loaf Bread.**—Sift together two or three times one pound of flour, three teaspoonfuls of baking powder, one saltspoonful of salt, and one teaspoonful of fine sugar; mix with enough cold sweet milk to make the dough of the consistency of biscuit; or, if you have no milk, use cold water. Work the dough only long enough to incorporate the flour well with the milk or water; put it into a baking-pan buttered and slightly warmed, and set it immediately into a hot oven; after about five minutes cover it with paper so that the crust may not form so quickly as to prevent rising; bake about three-quarters of an hour. This bread is sweet and wholesome, and may be eaten by some persons whose digestion is imperfect, with greater safety than yeast-fermented bread.

263. **Breakfast Rolls.**—Mix well by sifting, one pound of flour, three teaspoonfuls of baking powder, half a teaspoonful of salt, and one heaping teaspoonful of pulverized or fine sugar; into a small portion of the above rub two ounces of lard, fine and smooth; mix with the rest of the flour, and quickly wet it up with enough cold milk to enable you to roll it out about half an inch thick; cut out the dough with a tin shape or with a sharp knife, in the form of diamonds, lightly wet the top with water, and double them half over. Put them upon a tin, buttered and warmed, and bake them in a hot oven.

264. **Tea Biscuit.**—Mix as above, using the same proportions, and cutting out with a round biscuit-cutter; when they are baked, wash them over with cold milk, and return them to the oven for a moment to dry.

265. **Finger Biscuit.**—Mix as above, cut out with a sharp knife in strips three inches long, one inch wide, and one-quarter of an inch thick; lay them upon a buttered tin so that they will not touch, brush them over with an egg beaten up with one tablespoonful of milk, and bake them in a hot oven.

266. **Cream Breakfast Rolls.**—Mix as above, substituting cream for the milk in moistening the dough; cut them out with an oval cutter, two inches long and one and a half inches wide; brush the tops with cream, and pull them slightly lengthwise; then fold them together, leaving a slight projection of the under side; put them on a buttered tin, brush the tops with cream, and bake them in a hot oven.

267. **Breakfast Twist.**—Mix as for breakfast rolls, cut in strips three inches long and half an inch thick; roll each one out thin at the ends, but leave the centre of the original thickness; place three strips side by side, braid them together, and pinch the ends to hold them; when the twists are all made out, lay them upon a buttered tin, brush them over with milk, and bake them in a hot oven. A little fine sugar dusted over the tops glazes them and improves their flavor.

Hot rolls and biscuits should be served well covered with a napkin.

268. **How to freshen stale Bread.**—A loaf of stale bread placed in a close tin vessel, and steamed for half an hour will be completely freshened.

269. **Toast.**—But few persons know how to prepare toast properly. It should be made with the aim of evaporating from the bread all the superfluous water, and transforming its tough and moist substance into digestible food: for this reason the slices should be exposed gradually to heat of a gentle fire, first upon one side and then upon the other, for one minute, and after that they may be toasted golden-brown; at this stage it has become pure wheat farina, and is not liable to produce acetous fermentation in the stomach; besides, it will now absorb the butter thoroughly, and both substances will be in condition to be freely subjected to the action of gastric juice, and consequently will be digested with ease. Dry toast should be sent

to the table the instant it is made. Buttered toast should be set into the oven for about five minutes to render it crisp.

www.ingramcontent.com/pod-product-compliance
Lightning Source LLC
Chambersburg PA
CBHW081625100526
44590CB00021B/3600